TOUGH GUYS
OF THE BIBLE

LEARN THE TRAITS OF COURAGEOUS MEN WHO TRULY FOLLOW GOD

Paul Horrocks & Reverend David Horrocks

Published by Innovo Publishing, LLC
www.innovopublishing.com
1-888-546-2111

Providing Full-Service Publishing Services for Christian Authors, Artists &
Ministries: Hardbacks, Paperbacks, eBooks, Audiobooks, Music, Screenplays &
Curricula

TOUGH GUYS OF THE BIBLE
Learn the Traits of Courageous Men Who Truly Follow God

Copyright © 2021 by Paul Horrocks
All rights reserved.

No part of this publication may be reproduced, stored in a retrieval system, or
transmitted in any form or by any means electronic, mechanical, photocopying,
recording, or otherwise, without the prior written permission of the author.

Scripture quotations are from The Holy Bible, English Standard Version. ESV® Text
Edition: 2016. Copyright © 2001 by Crossway Bibles, a publishing ministry of
Good News Publishers.

Library of Congress Control Number: 2021915833
ISBN: 978-1-61314-631-6

Cover Design & Interior Layout: Innovo Publishing, LLC

Printed in the United States of America
U.S. Printing History
First Edition: 2021

To all the men of Christ Community Church who served God as great husbands, fathers, Sunday school teachers, elders, mentors, and youth group leaders.

CONTENTS

PART IV: THEY EXCELLED AT WHAT THEY DID

PART V: THEY FEARED GOD MORE THAN MEN

PREFACE

My father (retired pastor and graduate of Dallas Seminary) and I collaborated and wrote this book together. However, it is awkward to tell stories from two points of view. For simplicity, the overview of the men in the Bible and the key points are written from my perspective, and the profiles of other Christian men are written from his. We have labeled those as "Pastor's Log" throughout the book. In some cases, we have changed their names to protect their privacy.

Throughout the book, we summarize stories of men from the Bible. We highly respect the expository study of the Bible where you review a passage verse by verse. However, that's not the purpose of this book. We provide broad overviews of these men to highlight their incredible courage and hope that their stories will inspire you to go back and study those passages and these men's lives in greater detail. To make that simple, we included many endnotes (too many if you ask our editor) listing the relevant verses. It took a lot of work. We didn't just add them for extra credit, so please use them.

My father and I both have a dry sense of humor. If you read something in this book that sounds outrageous or ridiculous, that's because it probably is. For those of you who offend easily (you know who you are—actually, you probably don't . . . otherwise you would get help for that), we'll clarify our comic relief in the parentheses or footnotes, so please read them before emailing us to complain. You can email us at didyoureadthefootnote@wewillnotrespondtolazyreaders.com.

INTRODUCTION:
A CALL FOR LEADERS

Our nation is in trouble. As a people, we continue to turn further from God despite the overwhelming Christian influence that has blessed America throughout its history. Our nation is rejecting God in the legal realm. Our courts have repeatedly struck down laws inspired by biblical teaching while legislating the morality of the secular humanist[1] religion from the bench. Our national, state, and local governments have rolled back protections of religious freedom and replaced them with a cultural religion enforced by the government. Politicians publicly promote their faith in God to help win their elections only to reduce the commands of the Bible to something they "handle privately" once elected.

In the social realm, our culture has moved even further from Christian morality. The objectification of women and sexualization of young girls has reached overwhelming proportions. The worship of money, fame, and power dominates our culture. Millions tune in to watch TV shows about people who are famous for simply being famous and who have often become famous by doing something infamous.

Corporations mock God by promoting immorality in their advertising while siding with those attempting to tear down religious freedoms without any concern that people who call themselves Christians (and theoretically make up the majority of their customers) will stop buying their products. Many who call themselves Christians refuse to endure even the slightest inconvenience to put pressure on corporations that mock their supposed beliefs.

Even many churches have decided to cave to the culture to attract more members. Some simply change their morality to match the culture, while others avoid controversial biblical truths in the name of evangelism. The heavy lifting of true discipleship takes a back seat to "virtue signaling"

---

1. There are many definitions of secular humanism, but for the purpose of this book, it's defined as a non-religious worldview with a belief that humans can be moral and attain self-fulfillment apart from God. Secular humanists are generally hostile to Christian beliefs that conflict with anything that is popular in our culture.

that echoes the culture and fails to produce any real change in the lives of congregants.

What's surprising is that most people seem to know our nation is in trouble. According to a recent Gallup poll, only 21 percent of respondents are satisfied with the direction of the United States.[2] You have to go back to 2004 to find a time when that number exceeded 50 percent. I believe that our movement away from God and the resulting decline of morality has led to our nation's challenges. Most people agree that morality is on the decline. According to a Gallup survey, only 20 percent of Americans think moral values are excellent or good. Furthermore, 68 percent of Americans continue to believe moral values are getting worse. That number has exceeded 60 percent every year since 2002 when Gallup first asked the question.[3]

So if the majority believe our nation is on the wrong track, what can we do to change the direction of America? Throughout history, when nations have turned from God, He has raised up men to try to bring them back. The prophets of the Old Testament, the apostles of the New Testament, more recent Christian leaders, and ultimately Jesus have all performed this role. These are the *Tough Guys of the Bible*. The Bible shows us the characteristics of these courageous men. Given the state of our nation, men need to live like the Tough Guys more than ever. We need to act like them. We need to speak like them. We need to lead like them.

Some nations have heeded the warnings of these men and turned back to God, while others have ignored them to their own detriment. Some of the nations that ignored God have seen their power greatly reduced or have simply ceased to exist (I haven't seen a brochure for vacations to Babylon recently). We should not assume this can't happen to America. Our nation's move away from God has accelerated, and it's naïve to think there will not be consequences. A 2019 Pew survey showed that just over 65 percent of Americans label themselves as Christians,[4] down from 78 percent in 2007.[5] That translates to a 13 percent drop in just twelve years.

However, the Pew survey understates the scope of the problem. People were asked to self-identify their religion. That doesn't mean they truly believe it or adhere to its tenets. I self-identify as a Philadelphia 76ers fan, but don't ask me to name any players because I haven't attended a game since . . . whenever Dr. J was there. While 65 percent of the people in our nation call themselves Christians, that doesn't mean they attend church or

2. https://news.gallup.com/poll/1669/general-mood-country.aspx
3. https://news.gallup.com/poll/1681/moral-issues.aspx
4. https://www.pewforum.org/2019/10/17/in-u-s-decline-of-christianity-continues-at-rapid-pace/
5. http://www.pewforum.org/2015/05/12/americas-changing-religious-landscape/

conform their beliefs and actions to the Bible. A much smaller group truly follows Jesus.

In 1992, George Gallup and Timothy Jones attempted to quantify this group of saints and concluded they represented just 13 percent of the country.[6] Without even conducting any research, I think it's safe to assume this group hasn't grown since the 90s. In all likelihood, it has actually shrunk. Most who self-identify as Christians ignore the parts of the Bible that conflict with the culture.

The movement away from God is particularly alarming among men. Even though they represent roughly half the population, men make up only 45 percent of Christians but 68 percent of atheists.[7] You don't need a survey to figure this out. Visit almost any church in America on Sunday morning and you will see the women significantly outnumber the men. Volunteer at a charity, and the disparity gets even worse. It appears many Christian men have forgotten (or perhaps never learned) the biblical command to serve one another.

We could spend years researching why more men are abandoning God and still not reach a definite conclusion. However, I believe a significant factor is this: Men respond to strength and are not moved by a powerless gospel that lacks the capacity to change people. Preaching a gospel that says we must conform to the culture because we can't change it will never work. Let me repeat that for those who are hard of reading: Preaching a gospel . . . that says we must conform to the culture . . . because we can't change it . . . will *never* work! Men follow leaders and not followers. Christian leaders who cave to the culture will never inspire strong, competent men to follow Jesus. They may convince men to join them in a watered-down version of Christianity that permits them to continue living like the world, but they will not persuade men to deny themselves and take up their cross to follow Jesus as the Bible commands.[i]

Many Christian leaders would disagree. They find the language of the Bible harsh and believe churches and Christians need to soften their message and approach to appeal to more people. They emphasize the popular parts of the Bible and deemphasize the truths that offend. They accuse those who speak biblical truths boldly of being "political." Ironically, changing your approach and compromising your beliefs to build bigger coalitions is exactly what politicians do. More on that later.

---

6. George H. Gallup, Jr. and Timothy Jones, *The Saints Among Us* (Harrisburg: Morehouse Publishing, 1992), 13.

7. http://www.pewforum.org/2015/05/12/chapter-3-demographic-profiles-of-religious-groups/#gender-composition-of-religious-groups

I have bad news for those pushing this narrative. We're already doing this, and it's not working. Our nation has no shortage of seeker-friendly churches, and yet the number of Christians continues to fall. If Christians living like the culture or churches emphasizing the popular parts of the Bible led to more conversions and greater spiritual growth among congregants, *it would have happened already*. It's reasonable to conclude that the seeker-friendly approach hasn't led to a revival or a strengthening of Christian beliefs in our nation.[8] Instead, the culture is changing those churches as they modify their approach to make themselves "relevant" rather than challenging their congregants to conform their lives to the Bible.

Some of these churches teach you that it's easy to be a Christian. Men have been led to believe that you can become a Christian just by saying a certain prayer or by attending church some of the time. This is a false narrative. It's *not* easy to be a Christian; in fact, it's incredibly difficult. Yes, God wants you to say the sinner's prayer and repent; but after that, He wants you to go all in. He wants you to make Him Lord of your life and follow Him no matter how hard it might be. God created a way for you to spend eternity with Him by sending His Son to be the eternal sacrifice, but that act just made it *possible*. It did not make it *easy*. You still have to actually *follow* Jesus when the world puts tremendous pressure on you to reject Him. It's really hard to follow Jesus when you're getting that kind of pressure. Jesus made this clear to His disciples, and we need to make that clear to men inside and outside the church if we want them to become disciples as well. Men will rise to the challenge.[9]

While it's easy to get discouraged by the moral state of our nation and the lukewarm attitudes of so many men who call themselves Christians, what is encouraging is that we have great models for how we should respond in the Bible. The prophets, the apostles, and Jesus Himself never preached a powerless gospel. They challenged men to change their ways and conform to the commands of God. They didn't soften their message or selectively emphasize popular themes to make it more acceptable to their listeners. They clearly and unapologetically stated what the Scriptures teach.

What is even more encouraging is that these were solid men. If you met them, they would impress you. I believe some guys struggle with fully committing their lives to God because the media portrays Christian men as mean, incompetent, weak, or stupid. While uninformed and false, these narratives impact men's thinking. They want to be thought of as masculine and not weak or incompetent. Books have been written to show men how

8. If you want to explore this further, read Willow Creek's study on the topic entitled "Reveal Where Are You?"

9. For an overview of the gospel or resources to grow your faith, visit this website: lwf.org.

to live both Christian and masculine lives. However, they generally define masculinity using cultural standards. You can fish, hunt, grow a beard, and build muscles while still maintaining your Christian values—ooh rah!

This message misses a larger point. When you live out your faith boldly and serve God like the Tough Guys, it is the most masculine thing you can do because that is exactly what God designed you to do. He designed you to follow Him even when it's difficult. We should strive to live according to God's definition of masculinity rather than the culture's definition. In most circumstances, when you boldly live the way God designed, people will still consider you masculine even by cultural standards. The Tough Guys were not all hunters or body builders, but if you met any of them, you would never doubt their masculinity. You would marvel at their strength and courage. You would admire them.

This book focuses on four main characteristics of the Tough Guys. For each characteristic, we start by profiling two men from the Bible who demonstrated that characteristic in their lives. Then we lay out some key points on how to apply that characteristic to your life. After that, we profile two more recent men (some known and others unknown) who reflect these characteristics and lived like the Tough Guys. Some of them are men my father met in his years of ministry while others are men from recent history. Stories in the Bible are sometimes so dramatic and supernatural that it seems unlikely we would ever find ourselves in those situations (God has not yet given me the authority to call fire down from heaven or turn all the water into blood, but perhaps it will still happen). We show how the Tough Guy characteristics apply to these more contemporary men in situations more familiar to us. Finally, we look to the ultimate Tough Guy and show how Jesus demonstrated these characteristics. In the eyes of the culture of His day, He failed when they nailed Him to a cross. But we know that He won, and His was an act of courage and certainly not one of weakness.

For those who don't know Jesus or are exploring Christianity, we encourage you to evaluate Christianity based on the merits of the writings in the Bible and not on the behavior of weak men who claim to follow Jesus. If you want a model for what it means to live as a Christian, look at those who followed God faithfully and not those who followed Him only when it was convenient. Look at the prophets, the apostles, and Jesus. Look at the many saints who came after them and sacrificed everything to serve God and promote justice. Don't use the behavior of the weakest Christians to dismiss the claims of the Bible. Explore Christianity through the lives of men who gave everything to God.

For those of you who already believe the Bible, we hope this book inspires you to go even further in serving God. We hope you will adopt the characteristics of the *Tough Guys of the Bible* and help turn our nation back to God.

Women: We wrote this book to inspire and challenge men to live like the Tough Guys. However, there are plenty of courageous women in the Bible (e.g., Esther, Mary, Rahab, Ruth). We are not trying to overlook the courage and contributions of women in the Bible. It's just not the purpose of this book. It's a topic for another book. Stay tuned . . . .

PART I
TOUGH GUYS DEFINED

Chapter 1

WHAT MAKES YOU A TOUGH GUY OF THE BIBLE?

M any men in the Bible, and throughout history, had courage; but very few had the exceptional strength of the Tough Guys. The men that deserve the Tough Guy badge truly exhibited the kind of masculinity for which God designed us. These men chose to live for God despite tremendous pressure from other men to conform to the culture of their day. The Tough Guys had many impressive traits, but there are four characteristics that separate them from other men:

1. They took risks to serve God.
2. They spoke the truth directly.
3. They excelled at what they did.
4. They feared God more than men.

Let's define what we mean by each of these characteristics.

1: THEY TOOK RISKS TO SERVE GOD

The Tough Guys weren't afraid to take risks. They had the courage to face these risks because they had faith that God was in control. They understood nothing could happen to them unless God allowed it. Some of the more common risks they faced were the following:

- *Physical:* Many of the Tough Guys risked injury or death to serve God. Some went into battle as warriors. Others tangled with angry mobs who wanted to kill them just because they spoke the truth. Many of the Tough Guys challenged kings or governments who had the authority to execute them. Time after time, they chose to follow God despite these risks.

- *Social:* By speaking the truth, some of the Tough Guys made themselves very unpopular. Many people hated them. They frequently gave up the comfort of a community to serve God.

- *Economic:* The Tough Guys were impressive men. They were natural leaders who could have excelled in many different areas of the economy. If they lived today, they would have their pick of jobs in business, government, or media where they could have earned a lot of money. Yet so often they sacrificed wealth and prestige to serve God.

- *Freedom:* A lot of the Tough Guys spent time in jail, captivity, or exile. They often had to choose between following God's law or the predominant beliefs of their day. Despite the risks, they consistently choose God's law. While some gained their freedom, others died while still in jail or captivity. The stories of their lives on earth don't always have Hollywood endings, but all of the Tough Guys still chose to serve God.

2: THEY SPOKE THE TRUTH DIRECTLY

The Tough Guys told people what they *needed* to hear rather than what they *wanted* to hear. They didn't just speak truth; they spoke the *whole* truth. They didn't leave out the parts that were unpopular and just speak the "part of the truth" that was popular. They said *all* of what God had commanded them to say. This often made the Tough Guys very unpopular. A willingness to speak the truth when it's difficult is very rare in our culture (and probably rare throughout most of history). It's one of the many reasons the Tough Guys were so impressive and why we should try to emulate them.

3: THEY EXCELLED AT WHAT THEY DID

The Tough Guys had a variety of different roles, but all of them executed them exceptionally well. They were disciplined. They were proactive. They didn't wait for things to happen. They took the initiative and made things happen. They administered their roles very effectively. However, just because they excelled doesn't mean they were always successful. The Tough Guys had many setbacks. Despite the setbacks, they continued to faithfully serve God. They continued to use their talents as best they could in whatever situation they found themselves.

4: THEY FEARED GOD MORE THAN MEN

The Tough Guys believed God was the Creator and followed Him even when it was difficult. They believed in God's love but also in His judgment. They believed God could judge an individual but also a nation. They looked to God for protection rather than men. They followed God even when it was humiliating. While many men in the Bible show courage, they often hold back a part of their lives. The Tough Guys truly gave everything over to God. I believe this is the hardest criteria for the Tough Guys. It's possible to take risks, speak directly, and excel in your endeavors without truly giving 100 percent of your life to God. We need to follow the example of the Tough Guys and give everything over to God. We can't hold anything back.

While we found many men in the Bible who met these criteria, we chose to profile eight in this book. We also mention other Tough Guys but don't profile them. We're not suggesting that these eight men are the only Tough Guys in the Bible or even that they're the best. We chose them because their stories highlight how these attributes played out in their lives. Each of them faced difficult situations and had to make choices about whether to follow God or follow men. At different times in their lives, they all exhibited a willingness to follow God when it was costly. They truly lived Tough Guy lives.

Chapter 2

PUTTING THE TOUGH GUYS INTO HISTORICAL CONTEXT

Before 2500	Noah and The Great Flood
2081 BC	God's Covenant with Abram
2006 BC	Birth of Jacob and Esau
1898 BC	**Joseph** Sold into Slavery
1875 BC	Jacob and Eleven Other Sons Went to Egypt
1525 BC	Birth of Moses
1446 BC	Exodus from Egypt
1406 BC	Joshua Led the Israelites into the Promised Land
1169 BC	**Gideon** Led the Israelites Against the Midianites
1043 BC	Saul Made King of Israel
1003 BC	David Made King over All of Israel
970 BC	Solomon Made King over All of Israel
931 BC	Civil War Divided Israel into Ephraim and Judah
863 BC	**Elijah** Prayed for Drought
722 BC	Ephraim Conquered by Assyria
605 BC	Judah Comes Under Babylonian Control

604 BC	**Daniel** Interprets Nebuchadnezzar's Dream
537 BC	Jewish Exiles Begin Return to Judah
444 BC	**Nehemiah** Went to Jerusalem to Rebuild the Wall
26 AD	**John the Baptist** Called Judah to Repent
26 AD	Baptism of **Jesus**
30 AD	Death and Resurrection of **Jesus**
31 AD	Stoning of **Stephen**
34 AD	Conversion of **Paul**
48 AD	The Council at Jerusalem

Table 1: Timeline of Key Biblical Figures (All Dates Are Estimates);
Tough Guys in Bold [10]

Let's start with a brief history of the Bible (seriously . . . really brief) so we can put the Tough Guys in historical context. We included a basic timeline that you can reference throughout the book. Nobody likes to memorize dates. We wrote them down so you can save your memory for important things like Babe Ruth's lifetime batting average and your personal best max bench press (don't pretend like you don't know it).

Biblical historians disagree about some of the specific dates. We are not weighing in on that debate. We provided this timeline so you can put each Tough Guy into biblical and historical context. For example, we want to make sure you understand Elijah lived before Daniel but after Gideon and that Paul and Stephen were alive at the same time.

After God created the world, man sinned and turned from God, so He destroyed the world in a great flood. God saved only Noah's family, including his three sons and their spouses. After a period of time in which the world was repopulated, God made a covenant with Abraham that He would bless his descendants and give them a Promised Land. God reaffirmed this promise through Abraham's son Isaac and through Isaac's son Jacob, whom God would later name Israel. Jacob had twelve sons who became the twelve tribes of Israel. As a result of a famine, Israel, his twelve sons, and all their families, moved to Egypt to avoid starvation. We'll talk more about how they got there in the bio of Joseph.

Pharaoh (Egypt's ruler) gave the Israelites land, and they settled there; but eventually, a new Pharaoh enslaved them. (Talk about bait and switch. Beware of leaders with funny hats offering free land!) The Israelites lived

10. http://biblehub.com/timeline/#complete; https://www.jewishvirtuallibrary.org/the-two-kingdoms-of-israel

there for approximately four hundred years[11] until God brought them out of Egypt under the leadership of Moses and into the Promised Land (Israel) under the leadership of Joshua. Once in Israel, a series of judges led the twelve tribes for about three hundred fifty years. These judges were not like Judge Judy or Wapner. They didn't sit in a courtroom and try cases. They were a mix of spiritual, civil, and military leaders. God chose these judges and often raised them up to liberate Israel from people who were oppressing them.

Eventually the Israelites cried out and asked God for a permanent king to protect them from the people around them. God wanted the Israelites to trust in Him as their King and look to Him for their protection. He warned them that they would give up some of their freedom by having a king. (Rulers tend to make rules, which reduce everyone's freedom. For example, Israel had no taxes until they had a king. I bet the Israelites wish they had a do over on that one.) However, the Israelites persisted, and so God relented and gave them a king. First, He chose Saul. However, Saul sinned, so God chose David to replace him.

After King David died, his son Solomon became the king. After Solomon died, a civil war split Israel into two kingdoms: Israel, sometimes called Ephraim, and Judah. Each had their own line of kings. Ephraim had a series of kings who were all wicked and turned away from God. Judah's kings, from the line of David, were split between some who followed God and some who worshiped other gods. Ephraim and Judah frequently went to war with one another. Civil wars are the worst. No surrender is really ever permanent.

Both Ephraim and Judah had failed to heed God's warnings, and so He allowed them to be conquered by other nations. First, the Assyrians conquered Ephraim. Then, about 115 years after that, Babylon conquered Judah. The Assyrians and Babylonians took many Israelites home as slaves in their lands. The Babylonians later conquered Assyria. When the Persians conquered both Babylon and Assyria about seventy years after Babylon had conquered Judah, they allowed the Israelites to return home, fulfilling God's promise to end their exile.

Some of the Israelites returned home for a period of self-rule; but about two hundred years later, the Greeks, under Alexander the Great, conquered them. Over the next three hundred years, there were some periods when Israel was occupied and others when they had independence.

---

11. Scholars debate the exact duration of the Israelites' time in Egypt. For simplicity, we have used a common estimate. The purpose of this book is not to break new ground on biblical dates. We simply want to give readers a rough timeline so you can understand where the various Tough Guys fall in the history of the world.

The Romans conquered Israel about sixty years before Christ's birth. The Romans controlled Israel for the entire period of time covered in the New Testament. At the time of Christ's birth, King Herod the Great ruled Israel as Rome's appointed leader. Rome gave the Jews some local autonomy over religious matters, which explains why they had a ruling body (the Sanhedrin Council).

In New Testament times, John the Baptist announced the coming of the Messiah. He baptized Jesus, who went on to have a ministry for about three years until His death and resurrection. After His resurrection and ascension into heaven, His disciples preached the gospel[12] in Israel. As a result of persecution by Jewish leaders and the Roman government, many of them fled to other parts of the world and planted churches. The book of Acts captured the work and martyrs of many of the early Christians. The books of the New Testament cover a period of about one hundred years, ending with the Apostle John's prophetic vision in Revelation late in his life.

We will fill in more of the details in the background of each of the selected Tough Guys. We encourage you to refer back to this overview and timeline as we lay out each Tough Guy's role in the Bible.

---

12. For an overview of the gospel, visit this website: lwf.org.

PART II

THEY TOOK RISKS TO SERVE GOD

Chapter 3

GIDEON: RIDICULOUS ODDS, RIDICULOUS FAITH

| 1169 BC | **Gideon** Led the Israelites Against the Midianites |

BACKGROUND ON GIDEON

There was a frequent pattern in the Old Testament in which the Israelites would turn from God and do what was right in their own eyes. Then, God would give them over to their sin and allow another nation or tribe to conquer or oppress them. Eventually the Israelites would humble themselves and cry out to God, and He would raise up a leader to liberate them. After God liberated them, the Israelites would quickly turn from God and do what was right in their own eyes, leading to more judgment and oppression. Reading the Old Testament can sometimes be as frustrating as watching a bad horror movie. You scream at the girl in the high heels not to go into the abandoned warehouse, but she *never* listens!

Gideon was one of the leaders God used to liberate the Israelites during the time of the judges. Historians believe he lived about twelve hundred years before Christ. Most of what we know about Gideon can be found in the book of Judges in chapters 6–8.

The Midianites and the Amalekites were oppressing Israel.[13] To give some historical context, the Midianites descended from Abraham through his wife Keturah[ii] and her son Midian,[iii] and the Amalekites descended from Esau's grandson Amalek.[iv] In the Old Testament, it's not uncommon for groups that are fighting against each other to be descendants of the same person. (It's similar to the holidays when you fight with your cousins, but instead of using sarcasm and wet willies, they used swords and shields.) In this case, the Israelites, Midianites, and Amalekites all descended from Abraham, although he had lived hundreds of years earlier.

During the time of the harvest each year, the Midianites and Amalekites would come into Israel to destroy their crops and their animals. They were apparently trying to destroy the Israelites by starving them. After the Israelites cried out to God, the Angel of the Lord appeared to Gideon and told him that he should deliver Israel from Midian. Gideon initially protested that he lacked the capability; but after God showed him some miraculous signs, he agreed to lead.

God first commanded Gideon to knock down the altar that the men in his town had built to the idol Baal and replace it with an altar for God. When the men discovered that he had destroyed the idol, the Israelites wanted to kill Gideon; but his father protected him by pointing out that if Baal were truly a god, he should be able to defend himself (good thinking, Dad!).

God then sent Gideon to fight the Midianites and Amalekites.

But the Spirit of the Lord clothed Gideon, and he sounded the trumpet, and the Abiezrites were called out to follow him. And he sent messengers throughout all Manasseh, and they too were called out to follow him. And he sent messengers to Asher, Zebulun, and Naphtali, and they went up to meet them. (Judges 6:34-35)

The Midianites and the Amalekites had 135,000 warriors. Gideon initially assembled 32,000 men. Now 32,000 vs. 135,000 is not really a fair fight. Each Israelite warrior would have had to kill at least four warriors from the enemy to win a war of attrition. Those are terrible odds. You would not take that bet. However, the odds got worse. God told Gideon that he had too many warriors. God didn't want Israel to think they had delivered themselves. He wanted a smaller army to make it clear that their victory was from God. So Gideon told all the men afraid to fight to go home, and

---

13. To be more specific, Judges 6:35 says it was the tribes of Manasseh, Asher, Zebulun, and Naphtali who were oppressed by the Midianites and therefore banded together to fight against them. During the period of the judges, it was not uncommon for an outside nation or tribe to fight against only a portion of Israel.

22,000 left. (They may have been cowardly, but at least they were honest about it.) That left Gideon with only 10,000 men to fight against 135,000. This must have been discouraging. Each warrior would have had to kill 13.5 enemy soldiers to win a war of attrition. Even a group of ninjas wouldn't like those odds. But it got worse.

God told Gideon that he still had too many warriors. So Gideon instructed the men to drink water from a river. Of the 10,000, only 300 scooped the water with their hands and brought it to their mouths. Everyone else knelt to drink. God told Gideon to keep the 300 men and send everyone else home. God didn't want difficult odds. He wanted ridiculous odds.

At this point, Gideon must have thought he was being punk'd. God just reduced his army by 99 percent and told him to go fight 135,000 men. He must have thought God was sending him on a suicide mission. But it got worse. God told him to go sneak into the Midianite camp. However, God said, if he was afraid, he could take his servant with him.

Who wouldn't be afraid to sneak into a camp of 135,000 men trained to kill you? I'm not sure what good it did to take his servant with him. Even if your servant were Rambo, I don't think it would make a difference with those odds. Maybe if your servant were Chuck Norris . . . but I think most of the stories about him on the internet are . . . slightly exaggerated. Perhaps it's just nice to have a buddy with you when you think you're going to get slaughtered.

Despite his fear, Gideon went into the camp with his servant. While he was there, he overheard two Midianites talking about a dream one had that God had given Midian into the hand of Gideon. This encouraged him. He returned to his men and instructed them each to take a trumpet, a torch, and an empty pitcher and surround the enemy camp. When Gideon blew his trumpet, all 300 men blew their trumpets and smashed the pitchers which revealed the light of the torches. This threw the enemy camp into a panic. Most of the Midianites and Amalekites killed each other in the confusion while the rest fled. Gideon pursued the enemy and destroyed them. Three hundred men took on 135,000, and with the help of God, they won. This was the original 300, and it took place about 700 years before the Battle of Thermopylae depicted in the movie *300*.

HOW GIDEON TOOK RISKS TO SERVE GOD

Gideon took many risks to serve God and liberate the Israelites. God increased the risk with each command, and yet Gideon stepped up to each challenge. God first commanded him to tear down the altar of Baal. The men in Gideon's town posed a physical risk. The locals believed that Baal protected them. They were so dedicated to this idol that they wanted to kill Gideon. To be clear, they weren't blowing off steam. This wasn't like an exasperated father whose son just dented the family car, and in a moment of frustration, says, "I'm going to kill him." These men actually intended to end Gideon's life and would have done so had his father not intervened.

Gideon understood the risk since he destroyed the altar at night. While it would be easy to criticize Gideon for failing to do this in broad daylight, he still did it. He didn't back down from the command. Imagine if God commanded you to go to Yankee Stadium, remove the team name, and replace it with a sign for the Red Sox. I'm willing to bet you would wait until there were no Yankees' fans around to attempt that stunt. That's of course assuming that you would even have the courage to attempt it in the first place. Gideon took a significant risk in destroying the altar of Baal. That act alone involved more risk than God will ask most of us to take in our lifetimes. However, God commanded Gideon to do more.

Next, after Gideon assembled the army, he still faced tremendous risk. The Israelites had been raided by Midian for the last seven years. If they could have assembled an army capable of defeating the enemy, they would have done it already. The Midianites could terrorize the Israelites because they were too weak to defend themselves. When Gideon assembled an army of 32,000, it was still going to be an incredibly risky operation. The Midianites and Amalekites had camped against them; they were planning for war. Gideon couldn't use the element of surprise to flank them or use guerilla tactics to attack them at their weak points. The 135,000 men were assembled for war and were prepared for an attack from the Israelites. It took amazing faith for Gideon to plan an attack with an army only 25 percent as large as the enemy army.

When God reduced the army to ten thousand, it would have taken even more faith to believe the Israelites could win. Gideon followed God's commands even as the risk increased. After God reduced the army further to three hundred men, Gideon's faith, as well as the faith of those three hundred men, must have truly been tested.[14] The book of Judges gives us an indication of Gideon's faith earlier in the story. When the Angel of the Lord first appeared to Gideon, he questioned why God had initially forsaken them.

---

14. I'm not sure if Gideon or the three hundred men had more faith. Gideon had heard directly from the Angel of the Lord while the three hundred men had only heard from Gideon. These guys were *tough!*

And Gideon said to him, "Please, sir, if the Lord is with us, why then has all this happened to us? And where are all his wonderful deeds that our fathers recounted to us, saying, 'Did not the Lord bring us up from Egypt?' But now the Lord has forsaken us and given us into the hand of Midian." (Judges 6:13)

Gideon didn't question God's power. He believed God could deliver the Israelites but mistakenly thought God had abandoned them. Once Gideon understood that God was with him, his perspective changed. God's assurance gave Gideon the courage to go into battle with an army only 0.2 percent the size of the enemy army, carrying nothing more than torches and trumpets. He chose to believe that God was stronger than all those men and would deliver Israel. How often in your life have you been outnumbered and chosen to compromise on your beliefs to avoid a confrontation? If you're out with five other men from work, and they start talking about women as sex objects, do you speak up to challenge them or remain silent? If you're having a discussion about a hot button cultural issue with a group dominated by people who don't believe in Jesus, how quickly do you soften your views to avoid conflict? It's easy to rationalize our failure to take risks as Christian men when the numbers are against us. The story of Gideon should remind us that when we have God on our side, the number of those against us doesn't matter. If we're faithful, God can deliver us from any danger. We should never allow the size of the group opposing us to change our willingness to follow God.

Chapter 4

PAUL: RISKING IT OVER AND OVER ... AND OVER

34 AD	Conversion of **Paul**

BACKGROUND ON PAUL

Originally known by his Jewish name, Saul of Tarsus, the apostle began to use his Roman name, Paul, after his conversion to Christianity.[15] Educated as a Jewish Pharisee,[16] Paul lived in New Testament times when Rome controlled Israel. He persecuted the early Christians and had many thrown in jail. The first mention of Paul in the Bible is in Acts 7 at the stoning of Stephen, the first recorded Christian martyr. This occurred not long after Jesus had risen from the dead and ascended into heaven.

While Saul traveled on the road to Damascus in his efforts to persecute Christians, a light blinded him, and Jesus spoke to him out of heaven. This led to Paul's conversion. He went on to become one of the most effective Christian missionaries (if not the most effective) in history. He traveled the Roman world, setting up churches and recruiting many others to spread the

---

15. While he was Jewish, Paul was also born a Roman citizen, which came in handy a few times when he was persecuted.

16. The Pharisees were a strict Jewish religious party made up of scribes and laymen who believed God had given Moses a written law as well as an oral law that was passed down through generations and later recorded in the Talmud.

news of Jesus. He also wrote many letters to churches and individuals, and at least thirteen of them were preserved as books in the New Testament.[17]

Paul possessed incredible gifts from the Holy Spirit, including teaching, prophecy, and healing. Paul even raised a young man from the dead. (The poor kid had fallen asleep and then fell out of the window where he was sitting while Paul spoke.[v] I think it's only fair that if your preaching is so boring that someone dozes off and falls to his death, you should take the time to raise him from the dead. It's just common courtesy.) This is where we get the phrase *bored to death*.[18]

During his missionary journeys, Paul was whipped, beaten, and stoned multiple times. He was also frequently imprisoned (leaving him a lot of time to write letters) and shipwrecked at least three times. After his conversion, the Jewish religious leaders viewed him as a traitor and repeatedly attempted to kill him. Paul lived under constant threat of violence. While the Bible doesn't record his death, Paul suggested his life was nearly over in his last letter to Timothy.[vi] Historians believe that the Roman authorities eventually beheaded Paul not far from Rome. Paul's life stands as a testimony that God can change the hearts of even the most wicked men. It reminds us that God can use the most sinful among us to do great things.

HOW PAUL TOOK RISKS TO SERVE GOD

After Paul's conversion, he consistently took risks to spread the gospel of Jesus. When he switched sides from persecuting Christians to preaching the gospel, Paul took on physical risk but also made a tremendous social sacrifice. He gave up his friends as well as his connections to the ruling elite of his day. Paul interacted with the High Priest.[vii] He had access to power. It would be similar to having a key ambassador role in a presidential administration: you would be part of the inner circle; you would get invited to all the right parties; you would meet political leaders, business tycoons, and celebrities (I'm not sure who the Garth Brooks and George Clooney of the ancient world would have been, but Paul was on a path to becoming buddies with them); you would feel really important. It would be incredibly difficult to give that up when you were so close to all the decision makers. However, Paul abandoned these privileges immediately after his encounter with Jesus. Paul gave up a promising career in order to serve God but faced

---

17. If Hebrews is included, which some attribute to Paul, then he wrote fourteen of the twenty-seven books in the New Testament.

18. I actually have no idea where the phrase *bored to death* comes from, but I'm not opposed to starting non-defamatory rumors just to see how far they spread.

certain alienation from his friends and a loss of influence with the ruling elite.

Paul didn't limit his social risk taking to his old Pharisee buddies. He took social risk with his new Christian brothers as well. When Peter refused to eat with Gentiles, Paul opposed him "to his face."viii We don't know exactly how this confrontation went down, but the language makes it sound as if Paul got up in Peter's face, like a baseball manager to an umpire after a bad call, and told him off.

Peter was one of the original twelve disciples. He witnessed the transfiguration as part of Christ's inner circle. Peter would have been a rock star in the early days of Christianity, while Paul was the jerk that used to lock up followers of Jesus. You would think Paul would just be grateful that the other Christians forgave him after his past persecutions. Who was Paul to challenge Peter? Yet that didn't stop Paul from risking social alienation to speak the truth when Peter failed to live out the gospel. Do you have that kind of boldness? Do you challenge other Christians about their sin even when they have prominent roles in the Church or have followed Jesus longer? Paul's rebuke of Peter represents a great example of how Christian men, full of the Holy Spirit, should challenge other Christian men.

Paul endured many physical sacrifices to serve God. Since the Jewish leaders regarded him as an enormous traitor, their efforts to execute him were particularly aggressive. They probably felt about him the way Americans feel about Benedict Arnold—they wanted him dead. The leaders who already knew him made plans to assassinate him. In the cities where he preached, he often caused such a stir that the leaders who learned about him imprisoned or whipped him. Paul took on tremendous physical risk to preach the gospel. In one of his letters to the Corinthians, he listed his many trials.

> *Five times I received at the hands of the Jews the forty lashes less one. Three times I was beaten with rods. Once I was stoned. Three times I was shipwrecked; a night and a day I was adrift at sea; on frequent journeys, in danger from rivers, danger from robbers, danger from my own people, danger from Gentiles, danger in the city, danger in the wilderness, danger at sea, danger from false brothers; in toil and hardship, through many a sleepless night, in hunger and thirst, often without food, in cold and exposure. (2 Corinthians 11:24-27)*

The physical trials that Paul endured are hard to fathom. Any one of them alone would have been enough to scare most men away from missionary work. Receiving thirty-nine lashes even one time would be brutal. His enemies flogged him five times. Through how many of those trials would you have remained faithful to God? After your first flogging, would you have kept going? After your third flogging, would you have kept going? After your enemies stoned you to the point of death, would you have kept going? If you were shipwrecked and spent an entire day in the water, clinging to some broken piece of the ship to save your life, would you have kept going? Paul kept going. He never wavered in his faith. If you met him, you would marvel at his conviction and willingness to endure such pain to serve God.

What makes Paul's sacrifice even more compelling is that he was aware of the dangers and took the risks anyway. It's not as if after Paul survived a life-threatening ordeal, he thought to himself, *That was a close one, but at least it's over and it probably won't happen again.* On the contrary, Paul understood the risks all too well. When Ananias first visited him at his conversion, God said he would show Paul "how much he must suffer for the sake of [God's] name."[ix] Later, Paul addressed the Ephesian elders for the last time before leaving for Jerusalem where he knew further trials awaited him.

> *And now, behold, I am going to Jerusalem, constrained by the Spirit, not knowing what will happen to me there, except that the Holy Spirit testifies to me in every city that imprisonment and afflictions await me. But I do not account my life of any value nor as precious to myself, if only I may finish my course and the ministry that I received from the Lord Jesus, to testify to the gospel of the grace of God. And now, behold, I know that none of you among whom I have gone about proclaiming the kingdom will see my face again. (Acts 20:22-25)*

Paul regularly received prophecies from the Holy Spirit. He knew his fate, but he chose to go anyway. Some people say that it's easier to die for Jesus than it is to live for Him. Now, I think that's weak justification from wimpy men who are afraid to take any social risk, trying to justify their cowardice. In reality, risking death is more difficult than risking social persecution from the culture. In addition, many martyrs endured persecution, in some cases for many years, before their deaths. Paul didn't just risk death. He risked suffering and torture to serve God. If you had to choose between not getting invited to the right parties because of your faith or being flogged and stoned, I think almost everyone would choose the former. Physical agony and the threat of death trumps missing out on a party or getting passed over for a promotion pretty much every time. If you don't believe me, feel free to prove it by signing up to be a missionary to the parts of the Middle East hostile to Christianity.

Paul also risked his freedom to serve God. While in Romans 13 he instructed Christians to obey their earthly rulers, Paul was frequently in prison. It was, of course, ostensibly hypocritical that the guy who frequently spent time in prison lectured others on obeying earthly rulers. (How about practicing what you preach, brother!) However, Paul's civil disobedience in proclaiming the truth was justified by God's commands. When man's law conflicted with God's law, Paul refused to bend. He showed us a great example of what it means to love God more than the praise of men. He sacrificed his freedom and eventually his life. What was even more impressive about Paul was that rather than get bitter about his imprisonment, he saw God's hand in it and even rejoiced.

> *I want you to know, brothers, that what has happened to me has really served to advance the gospel, so that it has become known throughout the whole imperial guard and to all the rest that my imprisonment is for Christ. And most of the brothers, having become confident in the Lord by my imprisonment, are much more bold to speak the word without fear. (Philippians 1:12-14)*

Not only did Paul's imprisonment give him an opportunity to encourage and embolden others, it also gave him time to write many of the letters that are now part of the New Testament. Paul embraced risk, and God used him mightily to spread the gospel.

Chapter 5

KEY POINTS ON TAKING RISKS TO SERVE GOD

GOD OFTEN CHOOSES UNLIKELY MEN TO LEAD—HE MAY HAVE CHOSEN YOU

We learn from Gideon's story that God often chooses unlikely men for leadership roles. When God first called him, Gideon protested that he couldn't lead because he came from the weakest family in the tribe of Manasseh, and he was his father's youngest.[x] In ancient times, the oldest son typically received the most prominent leadership roles, but not in the case of Gideon. God broke this mold other times as well. God made Jacob the father of the twelve tribes of Israel even though he had an older brother—Esau. God told their mother, Rebekah, that Esau would serve Jacob. (Rebekah loved Jacob more anyway. When parents say they don't have favorites, sometimes they're just lying.[xi]) The Lord commanded Samuel to anoint David as the next king of Israel even though he was the youngest of Jesse's eight sons.[xii]

God doesn't necessarily need men who look like typical leaders in the eyes of the world because He can give them strength through the Holy Spirit. After Gideon protested, God told him that He would be with him,[xiii] and later the Holy Spirit came upon Gideon.[xiv] The Bible describes a similar pattern with David. As soon as Samuel anointed him, the Spirit of the Lord came upon David.[xv]

Don't underestimate the power of the Holy Spirit. God can give ordinary men extraordinary strength to accomplish great things. In Luke, Jesus warned His disciples that persecution would come but that He would give them the words at the right time to witness to kings and governors.

> *But before all this they will lay their hands on you and persecute you, delivering you up to the synagogues and prisons, and you will be brought before kings and governors for my name's sake. This will be your opportunity to bear witness. Settle it therefore in your minds not to meditate beforehand how to answer, for I will give you a mouth and wisdom, which none of your adversaries will be able to withstand or contradict. (Luke 21:12-15)*

The Holy Spirit has awesome power. What we see in Gideon's story and throughout the Bible is that you don't need to look like a natural leader in the eyes of the world to accomplish great things for God. You may not have the natural leadership abilities of most men. Maybe you lack confidence, or you have a soft voice. Perhaps your bench press maxed out at 135 pounds back when you used to be "stronger." You might even stutter like Moses.[xvi] None of these things matter if God has called you to serve Him and take on risk. The Holy Spirit will provide you the strength you need to succeed.

SOME TOUGH GUYS ARE DELIVERED WHILE OTHERS DIE HORRIBLE DEATHS

While taking risks for God will lead to rewards in heaven, the payoff during the earthly lives of the Tough Guys ranged from extreme wealth that would make Warren Buffet look middle class, and power that would make Vladimir Putin jealous, to senseless execution so your head could be used as a party favor. Some Tough Guys flourished on earth, while others lived in fear or endured unthinkable torture. Others experienced both ends of the spectrum during their lives. After Gideon conquered the Midianites and Amalekites, the Israelites rewarded him with great wealth,[xvii] and he lived to a "ripe old age."[xviii] In the eyes of the world, he achieved success and lived many years, enjoying the benefits of that success. Elijah spent a lot of his life hiding from kings who tried to kill him, but in the end, God took him up to heaven in a whirlwind before he died.[xix] Meanwhile, Paul suffered many beatings, imprisonments, and other trials, after which, according to tradition, the Romans beheaded him. He received no earthly reward of wealth or a private chariot ride up to heaven. There was no direct correlation between the Tough Guys' willingness to take risks and their pleasure and comfort here on earth. Sorry.

Throughout the Bible, we see the same pattern. Tough Guy obedience didn't necessarily result in earthly rewards. While David was eventually made king, he first had to spend many years living in caves, hiding from Saul who used his army to hunt him. God delivered Daniel from the lions' den but allowed Herod to execute John the Baptist. Jeremiah spoke the truth, and God protected him for more than forty years before (according to tradition) the Israelites stoned him, while God allowed the Israelites to stone Stephen at a young age. (If you're not familiar with stoning, it's like dodgeball, but with rocks, and you're never allowed out of the circle.) Joseph endured slavery and then prison before Pharaoh made him second in command in Egypt, while Uriah was executed on the orders of David, the very man Uriah had dedicated his life to serve. If you respond to the challenge to take risk to serve God (which you should), do not expect a worldly reward. God may bless you immediately, but He may also "reward" your courage with more suffering and trials in this life. Focus on your reward in heaven.

Here is an alternative perspective on this. It may seem unfair that men who risked the most often met untimely deaths. However, I'm not so sure they got the short end of the stick. They left this world prematurely to start eternity with Jesus even sooner than their peers. That may very well be the better half. The Tough Guys didn't have a death wish, and neither should we; but if God allows your death, He may be rewarding you more than you know.

ETERNAL REWARDS AND THE PROBLEM OF DISCOUNTING

We often think of risk versus reward in investing, but the same thing holds true in eternity. In Matthew, Jesus instructed us to think about rewards in a very different way than the world.

> *"Do not lay up for yourselves treasures on earth, where moth and rust destroy and where thieves break in and steal, but lay up for yourselves treasures in heaven, where neither moth nor rust destroys and where thieves do not break in and steal. For where your treasure is, there your heart will be also." (Matthew 6:19-21)*

If you serve the Lord hoping for worldly success, this life may disappoint you; but if you serve the Lord hoping for treasures in heaven, He will never disappoint you. If you take risks for God, He promised to reward you; you just may not receive those rewards until heaven. The rewards Jesus described were not limited to financial benefits. When Paul converted to Christianity, he certainly lost a lot of friends, and he may also have alienated his family. Jesus addressed this loss of family in Luke.

And he said to them, "Truly, I say to you, there is no one who has left house or wife or brothers or parents or children, for the sake of the kingdom of God, who will not receive many times more in this time, and in the age to come eternal life." (Luke 18:29-30)

While Paul may have sacrificed his earthly friends and families, God promised to reward him many times over now and in heaven. That promise applies to us as well. If we take risks to serve Him, God will reward us.[19]

Humans tend to value immediate rewards over rewards in the future. Even when the reward in the future is much greater, people tend to discount the value significantly. Many people would take one hundred dollars today instead of one hundred fifty dollars one year from now, even though 50 percent is a terrific investment return. They discount the one hundred fifty dollars in the future to the point where they value it less than one hundred dollars today. Said another way, many people put greater value on an immediate reward than a reward in the future that is worth significantly more.

That same principle applies in eternity. Many people discount the permanent treasures in heaven so deeply that they value them less than the temporary treasures on earth. If someone offered you one dollar today or one billion dollars in twenty years, almost everyone would take the one billion dollars. However, the rewards in heaven will be so much greater than we can even fathom today, and they will last for eternity; while the rewards on earth will only last as long as you live (which might only be a few more decades or years or months or days or hours or minutes or seconds). Despite this, people often take the one dollar today because they are so short-sighted.

The Tough Guys understood the value of heavenly treasures. They risked immediate rewards for greater rewards in heaven. Paul even addressed the comparison.

For I consider that the sufferings of this present time are not worth comparing with the glory that is to be revealed to us. (Romans 8:18)

Paul understood that his suffering was nothing in comparison to the glory of heaven that awaited him. If we want to live like the Tough Guys, we need to update our arithmetic and place greater value on the treasures in heaven than the earthly rewards that often dominate our thinking.

EVEN THE TOUGH GUYS GOT THE JITTERS SOMETIMES

Despite their incredible courage, the Tough Guys experienced fear. Gideon kept asking God for miraculous signs because he feared the

19. Paul lost friends but gained many Christian brothers and sisters. He also experienced the joy of leading people to Jesus, healing the sick, serving the poor, and growing closer to God. Christians may receive rewards in this life and in heaven.

Amalekites.[xx] Paul admitted his fear in his first letter to the Corinthians.[xxi20] Nehemiah felt trepidation when he had to ask King Artaxerxes for permission to return to Jerusalem.[xxii] Moses begged God to send someone else to confront Pharaoh even after God turned a staff into a snake and changed his hand to leprous and back.[xxiii]

We should never be afraid because God is always with us. However, if you've felt fear in the past or feel it in the future, that doesn't disqualify you from serving God. You're in pretty good company if you've been afraid to take risks for God. The story doesn't have to end there. You can still take risks and serve God in extraordinary ways. God can still use you mightily to do things great and small to further His kingdom. Don't get distracted by your failings. Get excited about the possibilities of how God could use you starting now if you fully trust Him and follow His commands.

TOUGH GUYS DIDN'T JUST BELIEVE—THEY TOOK ACTION

People often say that "actions speak louder than words." I don't know when this saying started, but James, the half-brother of Jesus, said something similar almost two thousand years ago.

What good is it, my brothers, if someone says he has faith but does not have works? Can that faith save him? If a brother or sister is poorly clothed and lacking in daily food, and one of you says to them, "Go in peace, be warmed and filled," without giving them the things needed for the body, what good is that? So also faith by itself, if it does not have works, is dead.

But someone will say, "You have faith and I have works." Show me your faith apart from your works, and I will show you my faith by my works. You believe that God is one; you do well. Even the demons believe—and shudder! Do you want to be shown, you foolish person, that faith apart from works is useless? (James 2:14-20)

Some people have misinterpreted this to mean that works are a requirement of salvation. However, James really said that if you truly believe and have a heart change, it will show up in your actions. You will demonstrate your faith by how you behave. If you told everyone that you believed that the sun's UV rays cause skin cancer, but you let your kids play outside all day in the middle of summer without coating them with

20. I don't know if this happens to you as well, but every time we read a passage from Corinthians in church, I can't help but think of Ricardo Montalban talking about "soft Corinthian leather" in his Chrysler Cordoba. Then I start to laugh a little, which sometimes distracts other people at church. If you have no idea what I'm talking about, check out YouTube.

sunblock, people would start to question if you really believed it. (Or they might think you're a terrible parent. Seriously, get it together and put some SPF 50 on that kid!) Nobody who truly believed that would neglect to protect his kids that way. The same is true with faith in God. If you truly believe, it will show up in your actions.

James made the point that believing alone doesn't demonstrate faith. The demons believed that Jesus was the son of God, but it didn't result in a change in their behavior. They still followed Satan. The Tough Guys truly believed in God and demonstrated that with their actions. If you watched Stephen challenge the Sanhedrin Council, you would know that he truly had faith. He wouldn't even have to tell you. If you saw Paul get flogged thirty-nine times and then wake up the next day and continue preaching the gospel, you would never question his faith. When Gideon took on 135,000 men with only 300, do you think anyone dared suggest that he didn't believe in God? Of course not. His actions made it clear. If you want to live like the Tough Guys, you need to go beyond saying you believe and take action that demonstrates you truly have faith.

CHRISTIANS STILL GIVE UP THEIR LIVES TO SERVE GOD TODAY

The Bible is full of stories of men willing to die to serve God, but that strength continues with many men living in our times. The opportunities to take big risks for God have not passed.

In the summer of 2014, reporters interviewed fifteen-year-old Deborah Peter about the death of her father, a pastor living in Nigeria near the Boko Haram terrorist group. Boko Haram had threatened to kill him if he didn't stop preaching about Jesus and even burned down his church. Despite that, he rebuilt his church and continued to preach. On December 22, 2011, men from Boko Haram came to his house, pulled him out of the shower and, in front of his two kids, demanded that he renounce his faith. He refused and responded to the terrorists' threat by quoting Matthew:

> So everyone who acknowledges me before men, I also will acknowledge before my Father who is in heaven, but whoever denies me before men, I also will deny before my Father who is in heaven. (Matthew 10:32-33)

They threatened him a second time, and when he refused to deny Jesus, they shot him three times. Then, they killed his fourteen-year-old son, Caleb. Deborah survived and eventually escaped to the U.S., where she has been able to tell his story.

His death may seem senseless. Many Christians may even think he should have denied Jesus just to protect his kids from the violence. Instead, he chose to trust God and follow His commands. While his death is tragic, his daughter has been given the opportunity to tell his story on multiple continents in front of governments and the press. Millions have heard this story of courage driven by faith in God.

Very few of us will ever have such a huge platform to proclaim God. There is no way this pastor from a small village in Nigeria could have understood how his willingness to take risks to serve God would be proclaimed to millions. He refused to deny Jesus simply because that was His command. He took risks not knowing whether any good would come from it, yet the evangelism through his death likely had a greater impact than his evangelism throughout his entire life. That's the kind of faith all Christian men should have. We should take risks for God and let Him decide how to use it.

Another interesting part of the story is that I can't find this pastor's name. I searched all the articles I could find, and none of them mentioned his name. They mentioned his daughter, Deborah, but just referred to him as a Nigerian pastor. This Tough Guy lived for the glory of God. Even though I can't find his name, you can bet the Lord knows him intimately. His story should inspire you to take risks.

There are many other stories of modern-day Christians taking risks for God. In its 2020 report, Open Doors estimated that 260 million Christians in fifty countries live under high levels of persecution. They also reported that 2,983 Christians were killed for their faith in the last year. That's more than eight people a day. Christian men in America should look to these men and women around the world as examples and inspiration for how to take risks to serve God.

SERVING GOD REQUIRES DYING TO YOURSELF

Anyone can follow God when it's easy. When surrounded by other Christian men at church or at a volunteer event, it's easy to live like Jesus. I've never attended a church event where someone pressured me to commit fraud or treat a woman like a sex object. The true test of your faith comes when you have to make difficult choices. How do you react when you have to make a real sacrifice? How do you react when following Jesus means losing an opportunity or enduring persecution? What choices do you make when you're not surrounded by other Christians?

Some Christians will say you should focus on the "main" things. They tell men to focus on the "important" things in the Bible and deemphasize the rest. This of course leaves open to interpretation what's a really important thing and what's a minor thing. This gives men license to make the areas that are easy to follow Jesus the "main" things and the areas that are difficult the "minor" things. For example, some men might categorize giving money to the church as a main thing but reduce maintaining sexual integrity to a minor thing. However, if you have a job where you make a lot of money, it's not really much of a sacrifice to give a small portion to the church, but in a culture that promotes unrestrained sexuality as a "right" or "freedom," it can be extremely difficult to maintain sexual integrity. Rather than focus on the "main" things, focus on the difficult things. If you can live for Jesus when it's difficult, you will be able to live for Him when it's easy.

Giving up your life for Jesus would certainly be difficult. If you were told to do something in opposition to God's commands or face death, it would take a tremendous amount of courage to stand your ground. I have a friend who grew up in Germany. We often talk about the horrors of World War II and what their leaders commanded German soldiers to do in the concentration camps. While many men believe they would have refused to follow the orders to execute prisoners, my friend and I both agree that we don't know for sure. I want to believe that I would have the courage in that situation to refuse the orders and risk death, but until I've actually been tested, I don't know for certain how I would respond. What I do know is that if I'm unwilling to take risks for God when the stakes are much lower (e.g., economic or social risk), then it is very unlikely that I would have the courage to stand my ground when my life was on the line. If you lack the courage to take small risks, don't kid yourself that you'll have the courage to take big risks. You need to practice taking small risks for God so you're ready to take big risks when the situation arrives.

As Christian men, we should have the courage to go to our deaths for Jesus, but it's unlikely that most of us will ever find ourselves in that situation. It's much more likely that God will ask us to take smaller risks such as social or economic sacrifices. In fact, you shouldn't think of giving up your life as just a physical death. As Christians, the Bible calls us to give up our lives for Jesus in different ways. The Bible commands us to put our old lives to death and follow Jesus. Baptism essentially represents the act of dying to your sin and being raised into a new life in Jesus. We're commanded to give up our own desires and choose a life that is pleasing to God. We're essentially asked to die to ourselves so that we can live for Jesus. This kind of death means seeing the purpose of your life in a whole new light. Jesus saved you from death so that you could live to serve Him.

One of the most likely risks you will face is social risk. Men often feel tremendous pressure to conform to the culture so that people like them.

When the culture and the Bible come into conflict (which seems to be happening more and more often), we have to put to death our own desire for cultural acceptance and follow God's commands. Too often, Christian men hide their true beliefs or de-emphasize them so that the people of this world will like them. They justify it in the name of evangelism. "If I get people to like me, then I will have the opportunity to tell them about Jesus." But we see that the Tough Guys didn't worry about whether people liked them. They were willing to give up their friendships of this world to follow God. The Apostle Paul certainly lost influence with powerful people after he became a Christian. He chose God over his earthly relationships. That is the type of risk most men in the U.S. will face. While we may not face a physical death as so many of the Tough Guys did, we must die to ourselves if we want to serve God.

THE HOLY SPIRIT GIVES US THE COURAGE TO TAKE RISKS

The Tough Guys weren't naturally more courageous than the rest of us. The Holy Spirit provided their courage. They spent significant time praying and fasting. They sought strength from God rather than trying to do it on their own. Moses spent many days in fellowship with God. On at least two occasions, he spent forty days on a mountain with God.[xxiv] In Exodus 34, when he received the Ten Commandments the second time, Moses didn't eat or drink for forty days.[21] When he came down, his face shone so brightly—because he had been talking to God—all the elders were afraid to come near him. He had to put a veil on his face so that the Israelites wouldn't fear him. Moses also pleaded with God to go with them into the land of Canaan or not to send them at all.[xxv] Moses understood that Israel needed God's strength to defeat their enemies.

King David also prayed to God frequently. He would ask God whether he should go into battle and whether God would provide victory. He knew he needed God's strength to win. David wrote more than seventy psalms. These were prayers to God in which David often poured out his heart. The Bible gives us glimpses into the prayer lives of many of the other Tough Guys as well. Elijah spoke to God frequently and even lamented because he thought he was the only one left in Israel who wasn't worshiping Baal.[xxvi] Daniel prayed three times a day.[xxvii] Nehemiah spent time praying and fasting before he asked the king for permission to go rebuild the walls of Jerusalem.[xxviii] In his first letter to the Thessalonians, the Apostle Paul instructed the early Christians to pray without ceasing.[xxix] The Tough Guys understood they needed strength from

---

21. While it seems impossible that someone could not drink for forty days and survive, we must remember that Moses was with God who could sustain him supernaturally.

God. They didn't rely on their own strength. They understood our weakness as men when we try to do things alone.

Many other strong Christian men throughout history accomplished great things through prayer. William Wilberforce played a significant role in ending the slave trade and eventually slavery throughout the British Empire. He prayed three times a day for an hour each time.[xxx] David Wilkerson, who started Times Square Church in New York City and launched other worldwide ministries like Teen Challenge, prayed constantly.[xxxi] George Muller was a minister who launched a mission organization and started orphanages in England in the 1800s. He and his wife gave away all their wealth and relied completely on God to provide money for all their ministries. He prayed so often that he tracked more than fifty thousand direct answers to prayer throughout his life.[xxxii] These are just a few of the examples of Christian men who sought God continually through prayer and accomplished amazing things through the strength God gave them.

If you want to have the courage of the Tough Guys, you need to spend time with God consistently and ask Him for the courage to live out His commands all the time. You can't just cry out to God in times of trouble. You need to spend time in prayer regularly to build up that spiritual strength. Every relationship works this way. If you ignored your friend for years and never returned any of his calls, but then when you were interested in a job at his company, you reached out to him for help, it's very unlikely that he would be inclined to help you. He would realize that you didn't want a real relationship and you only cared about how he could help you. God always wants a relationship with us, but building a relationship with Him requires an investment. You need to spend time with God if you want the strength to face difficult things.

Most Christian men in our culture don't spend much time in prayer.[22] Many churches don't even have regular prayer meetings, and those that have regular prayer meetings often have few attendees. Sometimes the church leadership doesn't model it very well by talking about prayer in their own lives. Jesus taught His disciples to pray by constantly doing it Himself, but He also preached about the importance of prayer.

> *And he told them a parable to the effect that they ought always to pray and not lose heart. He said, "In a certain city there was a judge who neither feared God nor respected man. And there was a widow in that city who kept coming to him and saying, 'Give me justice against my adversary.' For a while he refused, but afterward he said to himself,*

22. https://www.christiantoday.com/article/daily-bible-reading-and-prayer-is-a-struggle-for-many-evangelicals/36765.htm

'Though I neither fear God nor respect man, yet because this widow keeps bothering me, I will give her justice, so that she will not beat me down by her continual coming.'" And the Lord said, "Hear what the unrighteous judge says. And will not God give justice to his elect, who cry to him day and night? Will he delay long over them? I tell you, he will give justice to them speedily. Nevertheless, when the Son of Man comes, will he find faith on earth?" (Luke 18:1-8)

If you want spiritual strength, you should pray like the widow. If you want courage like the Tough Guys, you need to seek God in all things and not just when you have a problem. God will respond and give you the strength you need to take risks for Him.

GOD PROVIDES PROTECTION

The Tough Guys understood that their protection came from God. That explains why they had the courage to take risks with the odds stacked against them. They understood that having God on your side trumps all the men on the other side. Why did Gideon have confidence to take on 135,000 men with only 300? He understood God protected him. Why did David always ask God if He would give the enemy into his hand? He understood that God provided the victory. Why was Daniel willing to risk the lions' den to continue praying? He believed that God could and would deliver him. What gave Nehemiah the confidence that he could rebuild the walls of Jerusalem before his enemies attacked them? He knew God could protect him.

Sometimes even God-fearing men in the Bible would look to other men to protect them. Asa was one of the good kings of Judah. He initially feared the Lord. He removed all the false gods and commanded Judah to worship the true God of Israel. Under Asa's reign, Judah prospered. Later when Zerah from Ethiopia attacked with a million men, Asa looked to God for protection. God defeated the invaders.[xxxiii] After the Ethiopians fled, Judah took a lot of spoil (that means that they got a lot of free stuff after they won the battle). Despite this victory from God, when trouble came later in his reign, Asa sought protection from men.

Basha, the king of Ephraim, built fortifications to start a war with Judah. Rather than cry out to God as he had done previously, Asa took silver and gold from the temple and sent it to Ben-hadad, the king of Syria, so that he would attack Basha. Asa's plan worked. Basha retreated from Judah to defend against Ben-hadad, and Asa won the war. However, this displeased God. He sent Hanani to Asa to tell him he should have looked to

God for protection rather than Syria. As punishment, God said Asa would have wars for the remainder of his reign, which he did.[xxxiv]

It's so easy in our culture to rely on our own strength or to look to other men. Our country has been blessed with so much wealth, opportunity, and freedom, it's easy to forget that it's all a gift from God. We often look to other men to protect us in business or socially rather than God. Even when God protects us in one situation, we so often forget about His amazing blessings and look to men for protection the next time. If we want to live like the Tough Guys, we must constantly look to God first. In all things, we should cry out to Him for strength and protection rather than trust in men.

TO BE TRULY ALIVE YOU MUST BE WILLING TO RISK DEATH

To close out this chapter, here is a challenge Martin Luther King Jr. (MLK hereafter) gave in a sermon on November 5, 1967. He gave this challenge one year before he died:

> I say to you, this morning, that if you have never found something so dear and so precious to you that you will die for it, then you aren't fit to live. You may be thirty-eight years old, as I happen to be, and one day, some great opportunity stands before you and calls upon you to stand up for some great principle, some great issue, some great cause. And you refuse to do it because you are afraid. You refuse to do it because you want to live longer. You're afraid that you will lose your job, or you are afraid that you will be criticized or that you will lose your popularity, or you're afraid that somebody will stab you or shoot at you or bomb your house. So you refuse to take the stand. Well, you may go on and live until you are ninety, but you are just as dead at thirty-eight as you would be at ninety. And the cessation of breathing in your life is but the belated announcement of an earlier death of the spirit. You died when you refused to stand up for truth. You died when you refused to stand up for justice.[xxxv]

Serving God is the thing for which you should be willing to die. Most of us will never be asked to make such a sacrifice, but if you wake up every day willing to do so, God can use you in mighty ways.

Chapter 6

PASTOR'S LOG: RISKING IT ON A SMALLER STAGE

CHRIS: RISKING HIS JOB TO SERVE GOD

When Chris[23] came to faith in the Lord Jesus Christ, he was already a father to five children. He had no idea that in the years following his conversion, his faith would be tested through those children as well as through the successful career he had developed to support his family. He dealt with the sudden and inexplicable suicide of his youngest son and the permanent forsaking of the family by his oldest. These trials were met by a daily, sincere, and growing faith in the Lord. He continued to trust God even as his faith was tested through trials that would challenge any man.

Chris' faith was further tested when he faced an ethical conflict at work. The owner of his company announced to the sales team that to generate more profits they would begin to over-charge certain key customers by as much as 20 percent. Immediately the Spirit in Chris bore witness to his conscience that he could not earn a living this way. Chris did not want to deceive customers to generate an income. Fellow coworkers looked to Chris for leadership. He spoke frequently of his faith at the office, but if he went along with this deceptive billing plan, his frequent talks of faith could be seen as theory alone. His coworkers could conclude that his beliefs were empty words that he would quickly abandon if they required sacrifice. If

---

23. Pseudonym used to protect the individual's identity.

he went along with this deception, he felt his actions would not match his frequent statements about his faith; but if he failed to go along with the plan, he would place his job in jeopardy. He provided the sole income for his large family and had spent years building his career with this firm. Who could blame him for putting his family before these corporate customers? Those organizations probably had large budgets and would barely notice the additional costs.

On the ride home from work, Chris knew what he had to do, but he had to decide how to do it. So he prayed for wisdom. He slept that night at peace with what he believed was the Lord's answer. The next morning, Chris arrived extra early at work. He requested a meeting with the owner where he explained his dilemma. Here is a paraphrase of the conversation.

> *Mr. Smith, for several years I wanted to work for your company since you had the reputation of doing a good job at a fair price; I was proud to be your representative. But the change in policy you announced yesterday strikes at the very heart and soul of your company. And for what reward? For a minimum financial gain at a maximum loss of personal stature within the company and the industry. Personally, I must submit my resignation with regrets and hardships.*

The owner immediately reversed his decision and assured each employee that he was abandoning his proposed deceptive pricing policy. He would earn his money the old-fashioned way. He would earn it through hard work, fair costs, and great service.

While Chris took a significant economic risk that day, he felt peace with his decision because he had sought wisdom from the Lord and received a clear answer. His courage impacted the integrity of the entire company. Not only did he refuse to lie himself, but he also saved his coworkers from having to choose between lying and keeping their jobs. Furthermore, his courage was an amazing testament to his faith. Any coworker could see that his beliefs were not empty words but sincere convictions which truly guided his life. Perhaps God even put this situation in front of him so he would have an opportunity to demonstrate the power of his beliefs to other employees.

Chris' story represents a real risk that many people face. So often in our careers we are forced to choose between integrity and financial gain. While very few of us will be asked to take on 135,000 men with only 300, as Gideon did, or to confront rulers who want to stone us, as Paul did, many of us will face ethical dilemmas at work. In Chris' case, he didn't lose his job, and so he ultimately didn't have to bear the cost. What's important is that he took the risk and had faith that God would provide an income for his family. Even if the owner had fired him that day, God could have provided for Chris in other ways. Chris chose the path of the Tough Guys. Very few men have that kind of faith. As you face challenges, remember Chris' story, and take the risk to serve God, trusting that He will provide for you regardless of the outcome.

CARL: CHOOSING GOD OVER SOCIAL STATUS

As a teenager, Carl[24] moved to New York City with his family. When he started school, he quickly learned that he was the only Christian in his class. Not only was he alone in his faith, he found that both his teachers and classmates promoted a secular humanist worldview that was hostile to Christianity. His classmates would even try to bully him with profanity-laced rants on his social media pages. Despite this, Carl looked for opportunities to show others the love of Jesus.

One day, when his English teacher was out sick, the school had a group of three "substitutes" come in and teach the students about their transgender and homosexual lifestyles. This "lesson" had nothing to do with teaching reading, writing, or grammar. The school was clearly using public dollars to indoctrinate the kids with their secular humanist values. They went beyond just talking about their own experience and encouraged the students to "come out" as gay or transgender. As you can imagine, there was no discussion of a traditional view of marriage or gender in this or any other class.

Carl told his parents about the "substitutes," and they called the school. The school asked to speak to Carl alone. While his parents had concerns, they prayed for God's wisdom and then agreed that the school could speak to Carl individually. When he met with the counselor, Carl explained that he knew it wasn't realistic that the school would adopt a traditional Christian worldview, but he did expect that if the school was going to promote their secular humanistic views on marriage and gender, they would at least present the traditional views as well. The school agreed that they needed to be more balanced and instructed the teachers to give both points of view when teaching on those subjects.

Throughout the rest of his time at the school, the teachers didn't completely stop promoting their secular humanist values, but Carl found that they pulled back significantly on promoting that agenda. Carl took a risk to speak up for biblical values, and it had an impact. He wasn't able to get the school to promote a Christian worldview, but he was able to reduce

---

24. Pseudonym used to protect the individual's identity.

the amount of indoctrination his classmates received on values hostile to Christianity.

What's amazing about this story is that Carl was just thirteen when he took this risk to speak up. Carl suffered bullying and hostility from his classmates as a result of his views, but he still spoke up. Many Christians in our country refuse to speak up when institutions promote values hostile to Christianity. Carl's story shows that even one man speaking up can have an impact. What if every Christian father in our country spoke up every time their kids' schools tried to indoctrinate the students this way? What if every pastor in the country challenged them to do so? We could end this use of our tax dollars to teach hostility toward Christian values overnight. Carl took this risk in his youth. Christian men can learn a lot from the example of this courageous teenager.

Chapter 7

JESUS RISKED IT ALL FOR YOU

While the Tough Guys were incredibly impressive men, they were all flawed. The only perfect Tough Guy of the Bible was Jesus. He had all the characteristics of the Tough Guys but none of the weaknesses. He didn't have fear, like Gideon and Nehemiah. He didn't persecute people, like Paul. He didn't have doubts, like Elijah and John the Baptist. Jesus was the only perfect man to ever live because in addition to being a man, He was also God.

Many non-Christians (and sadly many Christians) think of Jesus as just a nice, humble man who loved everyone. Some even think of Him as weak. Jesus was humble, and He did love everyone, but He was not weak. He possessed incredible courage. If you had the opportunity to meet Jesus during His three-year ministry, you would have been impressed.[25] His strength would have blown you away. You would have marveled at His wisdom and compassion. The Tough Guy we should strive to live like the most is Jesus.

Jesus took many risks to serve God. One of the first risks He took was to come to earth in the form of a man. He took on all the weaknesses of our flesh so that He could walk among us and teach us how to live. Imagine having all the power of God and giving that up to become a human child. If you were the king of a country, would you ever consider becoming a peasant so that you could serve your people? Going from a king to a peasant

---

25. You will meet Jesus one day whether you're ready or not.

represents just a small fraction of the difference of going from God to man. Yet Jesus took that risk so that He could save us.

As a man, Jesus also took social risk. His half-brothers didn't believe He was the Messiah.ˣˣˣᵛⁱ In addition, He was unable to perform many miracles in His hometown because His neighbors didn't believe in Him.ˣˣˣᵛⁱⁱ How would you feel if everyone in your hometown called you a fraud? You can empathize with His brothers: How difficult would it be to grow up in an environment where the Son of God is your older brother? Your parents would always ask you, "Why can't you be more like Jesus?" Of course, Jesus never did anything wrong, so it would be impossible to be like Him—that probably got old. It would be wonderful to know Jesus, but it would be challenging to have Him as an older brother growing up. The good news is that we know that Jesus' brothers do eventually believe in Him because they were praying with the apostles after His ascension into heaven.ˣˣˣᵛⁱⁱⁱ His brother James went on to lead the church in Jerusalem and even wrote the book in the New Testament that bears his name.

We know Jesus took on great physical risk and eventually gave up His life. He knew the physical pain and suffering that awaited Him and yet He didn't back down.

From that time Jesus began to show his disciples that he must go to Jerusalem and suffer many things from the elders and chief priests and scribes, and be killed, and on the third day be raised. (Matthew 16:21)

Jesus understood clearly what would happen and yet He didn't run away. He faced the task put in front of Him without fear. In addition, the idea that Jesus would have to die was not just a prophecy He received. Many people sought to kill Him long before Pilate ordered Him crucified. Even the people from His hometown tried to throw Him off a cliff.

But in truth, I tell you, there were many widows in Israel in the days of Elijah, when the heavens were shut up three years and six months, and a great famine came over all the land, and Elijah was sent to none of them but only to Zarephath, in the land of Sidon, to a woman who was a widow. And there were many lepers in Israel in the time of the prophet Elisha, and none of them was cleansed, but only Naaman the Syrian. When they heard these things, all in the synagogue were filled with wrath. And they rose up and drove him [Jesus] out of the town and brought him to the brow of the hill on which their town was built, so that they could throw him down the cliff. But passing through their midst, he went away. (Luke 4:25-30)

Can you imagine if all your neighbors got so upset by what you said they decided to throw you off a cliff? There are some kids growing up I would have liked to throw off a cliff, but I never actually tried to do it. If it happened, you might think you live in the wrong neighborhood, but this was not an isolated event for Jesus. The Pharisees plotted to kill Jesus because He healed a guy on the Sabbath. That's a fairly harsh punishment for helping a guy out.

He went on from there and entered their synagogue. And a man was there with a withered hand. And they asked him, "Is it lawful to heal on the Sabbath?"—so that they might accuse him. He said to them, "Which one of you who has a sheep, if it falls into a pit on the Sabbath, will not take hold of it and lift it out? Of how much more value is a man than a sheep! So it is lawful to do good on the Sabbath." Then he said to the man, "Stretch out your hand." And the man stretched it out, and it was restored, healthy like the other. But the Pharisees went out and conspired against him, how to destroy him. (Matthew 12:9-14)

The English Standard Version says "how to destroy" Jesus, but the New International Version translates that as "how they might kill Jesus." The point is that Jesus knew men planned to kill Him and yet He went to Jerusalem to face them anyway. Jesus saw this not just as an act of courage but also as an act of leadership and love. Jesus explained to His disciples that He chose to sacrifice Himself willingly.

I am the good shepherd. The good shepherd lays down his life for the sheep. He who is a hired hand and not a shepherd, who does not own the sheep, sees the wolf coming and leaves the sheep and flees, and the wolf snatches them and scatters them. He flees because he is a hired hand and cares nothing for the sheep. I am the good shepherd. I know my own and my own know me, just as the Father knows me and I know the Father; and I lay down my life for the sheep. And I have other sheep that are not of this fold. I must bring them also, and they will listen to my voice. So there will be one flock, one shepherd. For this reason the Father loves me, because I lay down my life that I may take it up again. No one takes it from me, but I lay it down of my own accord. I have authority to lay it down, and I have authority to take it up again. This charge I have received from my Father." (John 10:11-18)

Jesus reinforced this later when He explained why this was the greatest act of love.

Greater love has no one than this, that someone lay down his life for his friends. (John 15:13)

Jesus was the ultimate Tough Guy, and He made the ultimate sacrifice so that we could live. We are called to live like Jesus. If you want to live like Him, you have to be willing to take risks and sacrifice to serve God.

PART III

THEY SPOKE THE TRUTH DIRECTLY

Chapter 8

DANIEL: SPEAKING UP IN A FOREIGN LAND

| 604 BC | **Daniel** Interprets Nebuchadnezzar's Dream |

BACKGROUND ON DANIEL

A child of one of the noble families of Israel, Daniel's life overlapped with Jeremiah and Ezekiel. When Daniel was still a youth, Nebuchadnezzar carried him and more than three thousand other Judeans off to Babylon when he conquered Judah, as Jeremiah had prophesied.[xxxix] Nebuchadnezzar put Daniel and other young, intelligent, and discerning nobles into civil service training in Babylon. The Babylonian commander of officials changed Daniel's name to Belteshazzar, a name sometimes used in the Bible to identify him.[xl]

Most of what we know about Daniel comes from the book bearing his name, which he wrote. As a trainee for civil service, he first distinguished himself by refusing to eat the king's food (which he felt would defile him) and requesting that his group of trainees eat only water and vegetables. *You read that right.* Daniel only wanted vegetables. His buddies were probably pretty upset at this request, but after ten days, his group looked stronger than all the others, and so they were allowed to continue this diet. (I am sure this wouldn't be true for me, which is why I have never tried it.)[xli]

After Daniel entered the king's personal service, Nebuchadnezzar had a dream he didn't understand and threatened to kill all his advisors if they could not tell him both the dream and the interpretation. God revealed both to Daniel, and he explained it to Nebuchadnezzar. As a result, the king put Daniel in charge of the province of Babylon.[xlii] Daniel later interpreted a second dream for Nebuchadnezzar, and later still, interpreted handwriting on the wall for his grandson[26] Belshazzar. (It can be confusing that Daniel's Babylonian name is Belteshazzar and Nebuchadnezzar's grandson is named Belshazzar. If Daniel was a rapper, he probably would have called himself B 2 the Shazzar.)

After Babylon was conquered by the Medes and Persians, Darius became king. Darius had great confidence in Daniel and planned to make him the leader over the entire kingdom. The other leaders in Darius' administration despised Daniel because of his effectiveness (sounds like a lot of corporate bureaucrats I've met). They conspired against him but couldn't identify anything he had done wrong. (How many leaders in our country do you think could stand up to that kind of scrutiny?)

> *Then the high officials and the satraps sought to find a ground for complaint against Daniel with regard to the kingdom, but they could find no ground for complaint or any fault, because he was faithful, and no error or fault was found in him. Then these men said, "We shall not find any ground for complaint against this Daniel unless we find it in connection with the law of his God."* (Daniel 6:4-5)

To trap Daniel, the officials had the king sign a decree that people could only pray to Darius and no other god for thirty days. Despite this, Daniel continued to pray three times a day to God. The other leaders, who already knew Daniel prayed three times a day, told this to Darius, who felt he had no choice but to execute Daniel since he signed the decree. Darius had Daniel thrown into a lions' den, but God protected him all night. After a sleepless night, Darius went to the lions' den and found Daniel alive. He removed Daniel from the lions' den and had the men who accused him and their families thrown in instead. The lions killed them before they hit the floor.[xliii] (In ancient times, the rulers often executed a man's entire family as punishment for his crime. This truly proves that love does not conquer all. I apologize for bursting the bubble of every teenager reading this book, but it's probably better that you hear it from me.)

---

26. Belshazzar was likely Nebuchadnezzar's grandson. The Bible sometimes uses the word *son* to describe a descendant who may have been born one or more generations later.

Daniel went on to have several visions which foretold many historical events that came true. As far as we know, he died in Babylon. His life was an amazing testament to courage and to faith in God.

HOW DANIEL SPOKE THE TRUTH DIRECTLY

After Daniel interpreted his first dream, Nebuchadnezzar later called him to interpret another. Daniel explained this vision that prophesied judgment against the king:

> *"[T]his is the interpretation, O king: It is a decree of the Most High, which has come upon my lord the king, that you shall be driven from among men, and your dwelling shall be with the beasts of the field. You shall be made to eat grass like an ox, and you shall be wet with the dew of heaven, and seven periods of time shall pass over you, till you know that the Most High rules the kingdom of men and gives it to whom he will. And as it was commanded to leave the stump of the roots of the tree, your kingdom shall be confirmed for you from the time that you know that Heaven rules. Therefore, O king, let my counsel be acceptable to you: break off your sins by practicing righteousness, and your iniquities by showing mercy to the oppressed, that there may perhaps be a lengthening of your prosperity." (Daniel 4:24-27)*

It must have been terrifying for Daniel to explain the vision. While Daniel won the trust of the king with his previous dream interpretation, he was still a slave in a foreign land. Nebuchadnezzar could have him executed for any reason. Since Daniel already knew from the previous dream the king was willing to kill all his advisors, he would have been all too aware that Nebuchadnezzar would not hesitate to execute just one. Plus, this was a humiliating vision. The king was going to become like a lowly farm animal. That's not a message most monarchs want to hear, which explains why Daniel was initially alarmed.[xliv] Despite his concern, he gave the king all the details. He could have softened up the interpretation so the punishment didn't sound so harsh. He could have just said God would drive him from his kingdom for a while and skipped the part where he ate grass like an animal, but Daniel gave the king *all* the details.

It would also have been tempting for Daniel to stop at the end of the interpretation. He didn't have to give a recommendation, but *he did*. Daniel counseled Nebuchadnezzar to end his sinning and practice righteousness. That was incredibly bold given Daniel's position as a conquered slave! Daniel challenged Nebuchadnezzar to repent and change his ways. He attempted to save the king from this humiliation.

At this point, Babylon had conquered Israel.[27] Most Israelites would have wanted God to judge Nebuchadnezzar and send him into the fields with the animals. Nobody would have blamed Daniel if he told the king, "I advise you to just keep doing what you're doing. Don't change a thing. You're an awesome king. I'm sure it will work out just fine." Then, he could have watched while Nebuchadnezzar went insane. However, Daniel spoke the truth. He didn't return wickedness with more wickedness. He spoke the truth and let God manage the outcome.

Twelve months elapsed before the prophecy came true.[xlv] That would have been a long year for Daniel. Before it happened, how many times do you think Nebuchadnezzar doubted Daniel's interpretation? How many times do you think Daniel was asked whether he was certain about his interpretation? What appeared to be a false alarm could have hurt Daniel's reputation or led to a loss of privilege. After the stress of that experience, many men would have resolved to never prophesy again, but not B 2 the Shazzar. Many years later, Belshazzar summoned Daniel who spoke the truth directly again.

During a party, Belshazzar used the gold and silver cups stolen from the temple in Jerusalem as wine glasses. He and his guests intentionally mocked God.

They drank wine and praised the gods of gold and silver, bronze, iron, wood, and stone. (Daniel 5:4)

Apparently, God had about enough of Belshazzar because he had a giant hand write something on the wall. This was just a hand all alone. It wasn't connected to a person. As you can imagine, this terrified Belshazzar. He called all his wise men and offered to make anyone who could interpret the writing the third ruler in the kingdom.[28] But nobody could read the writing. So the king's mother suggested they call Daniel. (Even if you're the king, you should still listen to your mother.)

Daniel must have gotten even bolder in his old age because he challenged Belshazzar about his sin before he made the interpretation.

---

27. Assyria conquered the northern tribes of Israel, but Babylon later conquered Assyria, so all of Israel (Judah and Ephraim) would have been under Babylonian control.

28. According to Babylonian history, Belshazzar was the son of Nabonidus, who was the son of Nebuchadnezzar. It's likely that Nabonidus was still the king and Belshazzar was a co-regent with him. That would explain why Belshazzar offered to make anyone who interpreted the handwriting the third ruler and not the second.

O king, the Most High God gave Nebuchadnezzar your father kingship and greatness and glory and majesty. And because of the greatness that he gave him, all peoples, nations, and languages trembled and feared before him. Whom he would, he killed, and whom he would, he kept alive; whom he would, he raised up, and whom he would, he humbled. But when his heart was lifted up and his spirit was hardened so that he dealt proudly, he was brought down from his kingly throne, and his glory was taken from him. He was driven from among the children of mankind, and his mind was made like that of a beast, and his dwelling was with the wild donkeys. He was fed grass like an ox, and his body was wet with the dew of heaven, until he knew that the Most High God rules the kingdom of mankind and sets over it whom he will. And you his son, Belshazzar, have not humbled your heart, though you knew all this, but you have lifted up yourself against the Lord of heaven. And the vessels of his house have been brought in before you, and you and your lords, your wives, and your concubines have drunk wine from them. And you have praised the gods of silver and gold, of bronze, iron, wood, and stone, which do not see or hear or know, but the God in whose hand is your breath, and whose are all your ways, you have not honored. (Daniel 5:18-23)

B 2 the Shazzar scolded him like a schoolboy, likely saying this in front of all the king's advisors and wise men so they could hear the interpretation and evaluate whether they agreed. Daniel's harsh words would have humiliated the king, but this didn't deter him. Daniel called out Belshazzar specifically for not humbling himself before God. He didn't say he was a bad ruler or an incompetent leader. He said the king opposed the true God by drinking from the cups from the temple. Daniel went on to interpret the handwriting.

"Then from his presence the hand was sent, and this writing was inscribed. And this is the writing that was inscribed: Mene, Mene, Tekel, and Parsin. This is the interpretation of the matter: Mene, God has numbered the days of your kingdom and brought it to an end; Tekel, you have been weighed in the balances and found wanting; Peres, your kingdom is divided and given to the Medes and Persians." (Daniel 5:24-28)

Belshazzar responded by giving him a purple robe and gold necklace as well as making him the third ruler of Babylon as he had promised.[xlvi] With an interpretation like that, it's surprising that Belshazzar didn't have him killed. It was the night of the party, so the king might have been drunk. However, even under the influence, you typically don't reward people for predicting the end of your kingdom. As with Daniel's previous interpretations, this one came to pass. Belshazzar was slain that night and Darius the Mede took over the Babylonian kingdom.[xlvii] Daniel spoke boldly throughout his life, and God guided his path. His story inspires us to speak the truth directly and trust God to protect us.

Chapter 9

JOHN THE BAPTIST: SPEAKING UP WHEN YOUR HEAD IS ON THE LINE

26 AD	**John the Baptist** Called Judah to Repent

BACKGROUND ON JOHN THE BAPTIST (JTB)

At the beginning of the New Testament, the Roman Empire controlled Israel, and King Herod the Great had been appointed as the local ruler. John the Baptist, one of the few men in the Bible with a last name, was a relative of Jesus (just kidding about the last name). I'll call him JTB hereafter to distinguish him from the other Johns in the Bible. He was born about six months before Jesus to a priest named Zacharias and his wife Elizabeth. The angel Gabriel announced his birth and told Zacharias that JTB would call Israel to repent and prepare the way for the coming Messiah.[xlviii]

After JTB grew up, he lived in the wilderness outside of Jerusalem where he survived by eating locusts and wild honey (a true bachelor's diet—no preparation required). He called Israel to repent, and he baptized people in the Jordan River, but he kept the focus on Jesus. He told the people that One greater than he was coming. When Jesus launched His ministry shortly after that, He began by asking JTB to baptize Him.

TOUGH GUYS OF THE BIBLE

Herod Antipas (Herod the Great's son—hereafter referred to just as Herod)[29] later arrested JTB because he told him it was unlawful that the king had married his brother's wife, Herodias.[xlix] (It's not only sinful, it makes Thanksgiving really awkward.) Herod wanted to kill John, but he feared his followers might riot because they believed John was a prophet, so the king kept JTB in prison.[l] Later, at Herod's birthday party, Herodias' daughter danced for him, and he vowed to give her anything she wanted. With prodding from her mother, she asked for JTB's head on a platter. Herod didn't want to be embarrassed at his party, so he had JTB executed. (That's a pretty strange party favor to take home. I doubt many men wanted to marry Herodias' daughter after that. "Come see all the stuffed animals I had as a kid and my collection of severed heads.")

The Bible doesn't go into great detail about the life of JTB, but from what we know about him, he clearly gave his whole life to God. He delivered difficult messages to Israel and prepared the way for Jesus. His life was a great example of a man who was both humble and bold. JTB was humble enough to declare himself unworthy to untie Jesus' sandal but bold enough to challenge the leaders of his day.[li]

HOW JTB SPOKE THE TRUTH DIRECTLY

JTB was so direct in his language that Herod cut his life short. While many believed him, his bold proclamations of coming judgment made him enemies. JTB challenged the Pharisees and Sadducees who came out to hear him preach.

> But when he saw many of the Pharisees and Sadducees coming to his baptism, he said to them, "You brood of vipers! Who warned you to flee from the wrath to come? Bear fruit in keeping with repentance. And do not presume to say to yourselves, 'We have Abraham as our father,' for I tell you, God is able from these stones to raise up children for Abraham. Even now the axe is laid to the root of the trees. Every tree therefore that does not bear good fruit is cut down and thrown into the fire. (Matthew 3:7-10)

The Pharisees and Sadducees were the ruling elite of their day. While Israel was controlled by Rome, Jewish religious leaders had some local authority, especially in religious matters. They would have been powerful people that you typically didn't want to offend. Despite that, JTB called

---

29. Herod Antipas did not rule as much of Israel as his father, Herod the Great. He ruled the regions of Galilee and Perea. By the time of JTB's ministry, Pontius Pilate ruled Judea.

them a "brood of vipers!" That's pretty direct. If you call someone a "snake," they understand it's not a compliment. Most people would be pretty offended by this. If you were pulled over by a police officer, you wouldn't call him a "snake" unless you really wanted a ticket. You would call him "Sir" or "Officer" and act incredibly respectful. That's just to avoid a speeding ticket. The Jewish leaders could do a lot more than give you a ticket. Most people would have avoided challenging them, but not JTB. He called out the powerful of his day.

JTB challenged men even when facing death. He understood Herod had the power to execute him, yet he still used direct language. JTB told Herod his marriage was unlawful.

> For Herod had seized John and bound him and put him in prison for the sake of Herodias, his brother Philip's wife, because John had been saying to him, "It is not lawful for you to have her." (Matthew 14:3-4)

When you call a man's marriage sinful, he doesn't generally take it well. What's impressive is that JTB didn't soften his language. He just stated clearly that Herod was doing something unlawful according to the Jewish religion. So often when we have to deliver difficult messages, we soften the language or even omit things so that the person we're speaking to is less likely to get angry with us. JTB didn't do this. He didn't say to Herod, "Hey, buddy, the Lord sort of wanted me to tell you that He's a little unhappy with your . . . matrimonial situation. He would have preferred that you marry someone a little less . . . already married. But this is just what the Lord told me. I'm a big fan of yours. I'm just trying to, you know, help you out and tell you what God is saying because I think it's in your best interest because He did create the world and is all powerful. And I'm just the messenger. I'm just saying what I was told. I'm not trying to offend you. I hope we can still be friends because you're my boy. By the way, you look really tan today. I love what you've done with the palace. We should hang out sometime. Peace out."

JTB didn't soften anything; he just said it directly. That's one of the reasons he was so effective. He didn't leave doubt in anyone's mind as to what he meant; he was crystal clear. When you challenge other Christian men about their sin, can you say the same thing? Are you clear when you speak to them? JTB's life is a great example of how Christian men should proclaim the truth boldly and clearly regardless of the possible repercussions.

Chapter 10

KEY POINTS ON SPEAKING THE TRUTH DIRECTLY

CHRISTIAN MEN CAN'T BE AFRAID TO SPEAK THE TRUTH WHEN IT'S DIFFICULT

Some Christian men would have us believe that we should only talk about the popular parts of the Bible so we can persuade our culture to join us. They believe if we win people over with popular biblical truths, they'll eventually figure out the difficult truths on their own. It's a little like treating a cancer patient for allergies and hoping he eventually discovers on his own he needs chemotherapy. The Tough Guys didn't behave this way. They spoke the difficult truths often at great risk to themselves. Don't forget that Herod beheaded JTB for what he said. Paul endured beatings and imprisonment for his words. Daniel risked death to give difficult interpretations to Nebuchadnezzar and Belshazzar. Moses went in front of Pharaoh and challenged him. The Tough Guys spoke to please God and not to please men.

If you speak the whole truth of the Bible, it's almost a guarantee some people aren't going to like you. If you doubt that, listen to the words of Jesus.

> *Woe to you, when all people speak well of you, for so their fathers did to the false prophets. (Luke 6:26)*

TOUGH GUYS OF THE BIBLE

If nobody ever gets upset with what you say, Jesus says you're a false prophet. You're telling people what they want to hear instead of what they need to hear. JTB called Herod to repent because he needed to hear it. Daniel challenged Belshazzar because he was mocking God. God has commanded us to challenge other Christians as well. Here are just a few passages on this topic:

> If your brother sins against you, go and tell him his fault, between you and him alone. If he listens to you, you have gained your brother. But if he does not listen, take one or two others along with you, that every charge may be established by the evidence of two or three witnesses. If he refuses to listen to them, tell it to the church. And if he refuses to listen even to the church, let him be to you as a Gentile and a tax collector. (Matthew 18:15-17)

> As for you, brothers, do not grow weary in doing good. If anyone does not obey what we say in this letter, take note of that person, and have nothing to do with him, that he may be ashamed. Do not regard him as an enemy, but warn him as a brother. (2 Thessalonians 3:13-15)

> My brothers, if anyone among you wanders from the truth and someone brings him back, let him know that whoever brings back a sinner from his wandering will save his soul from death and will cover a multitude of sins. (James 5:19-20)

The Bible commands us to actively challenge one another. It also commands us to treat each other as brothers. Our goal is not alienation but restoration. Sometimes it takes direct language to get men to listen (actually, it's most of the time). If you lack the boldness to speak direct truths to other men, ask God to give you strength in that area. Also, ask Him for wisdom about when to speak up and when to remain silent. The Bible says that if we ask for wisdom and do not doubt, then God will provide it.[lii]

In the Great Commission, Jesus commanded us to go tell people about *all* of His commands.

> "Go therefore and make disciples of all nations, baptizing them in the name of the Father and of the Son and of the Holy Spirit, teaching them to observe all that I have commanded you. And behold, I am with you always, to the end of the age." (Matthew 28:19-20)

Jesus didn't say, "Go tell them about the popular parts of my teachings and let them figure out the rest on their own." He said, "teaching them to observe *all that I have commanded you*." Jesus didn't give us the freedom to cherry pick which of His commands to teach and which to avoid. He commanded us to teach all of them.

You don't generally have to challenge Christians to talk about the parts of the Bible that are popular. It's easy to talk about forgiveness, loving your neighbor as yourself, and taking care of the poor. Since our culture agrees with those biblical teachings, those conversations are rarely controversial. It takes more courage to teach the commands of the Bible that conflict with our culture. It's not that you should overemphasize the parts of the Bible that are offensive. You just can't neglect them. I am not suggesting that you should only focus on sin and judgment. Let me say that again since some critics are hard of reading. I am not suggesting . . . that you should only focus . . . on sin and judgment. What I am saying is that you can't avoid those topics because they are difficult. You need to use your wisdom about when to focus on which topics, but check yourself and make sure ungodly fear is not driving you to avoid biblical truths that are offensive to our culture. Those are the truths that men may need to hear the most.

NEED A PERSPECTIVE CHANGE

Many Christian men hesitate to speak the truth of the Bible because they wonder, *What will happen to me if I speak up?* The Tough Guys had a different perspective. They asked, *What will happen to them if I don't speak up?* The Tough Guys regarded the fate of other men as more important than their own. JTB wasn't trying to criticize the people of Judah. He was calling them to repentance and trying to save them from judgment.

Daniel put Nebuchadnezzar's welfare above his own. He could have said to himself, *This guy conquered Judah and enslaved me. I hope he spends the rest of his life eating grass with the cows.* But instead, he cared about Nebuchadnezzar more than himself. He took a risk in challenging him to turn away from sin so that the king might avoid the judgment prophesied by his dream.

The Apostle Paul used some of the most aggressive language in the Bible to challenge the early churches who had forgotten God's commands. It's important to note he was writing to churches. He wasn't writing to non-believers. He was writing to those who had received Christ but were failing to live in a way that reflected Christ. Paul didn't endure the beatings, shipwrecks, and trials of his missionary work just so he could show how superior he was. He didn't write these things to make his readers feel bad. He knew that their sins were pulling them further and further from the Lord, and he wanted to save them from an eternity in isolation from God.

Even Peter aggressively called his readers to holiness in his first letter to the churches in Asia.

> *Therefore, preparing your minds for action, and being sober-minded, set your hope fully on the grace that will be brought to you at the revelation of Jesus Christ. As obedient children, do not be conformed to the passions of your former ignorance, but as he who called you is holy, you also be holy in all your conduct, since it is written, "You shall be holy, for I am holy." (1 Peter 1:13-16)*

Some churches refuse to call men to holiness out of a fear they might be labeled "unloving." However, the Bible gives us these commands specifically because God *does* love us. The Tough Guys wrote and spoke these commands out of love rather than anger. If you want to be like the Tough Guys, you need to change your perspective and start thinking about what will happen to other men if you *don't* speak up.

THE TRUTH OFFENDS MORE THAN LIES

A friend called me one night, pretty exasperated, and said, "The only thing that upsets my wife more than when I lie to her is when I actually tell her the truth." People are often most offended by the truth they don't like. We know that the Bible is truth, and parts of that truth are offensive to our culture. The fact that someone might take offense at the truth doesn't relieve you of your obligation to speak it.

God sent a drought to Judah to warn them about the impending destruction by Babylon, but the people failed to listen. Jeremiah interceded on behalf of Judah and asked God to forgive them, but He would not relent. God responded to Jeremiah.

> *Then the Lord said to me, "Though Moses and Samuel stood before me, yet my heart would not turn toward this people. Send them out of my sight, and let them go! And when they ask you, 'Where shall we go?' you shall say to them, 'Thus says the Lord:*
>
> *"'Those who are for pestilence, to pestilence,*
> *and those who are for the sword, to the sword;*
> *those who are for famine, to famine,*
> *and those who are for captivity, to captivity.'" (Jeremiah 15:1-2)*

This would have been an incredibly offensive thing for Jeremiah to say, but God commanded him to say it. Imagine that there was just an enormous earthquake and hundreds of thousands of people were left homeless. They come to you as a prophet and say, "Where should we go?" You respond by telling them that "because of your sin, some of you will get diseases, others will be killed by invaders, still others will starve in a famine—and even if you survive all that, you will probably be carried off to a foreign land as a prisoner of war." If someone made a home video of this, it would blow up on Twitter, and all the talking heads on TV would label you an insensitive bully who enjoys kicking people when they're down. Even when everything you said came true, no one would remember. They would just remember that it was offensive at the time you said it. Sadly, if instead you told everyone that you felt their pain and everything would work out, nobody would care later when you were completely wrong.

Many would rather hear the false reassurance of lies than the offense of the truth. That reality will not change until Jesus returns. Until then, the truth will often be met with condemnation and offense. Do not let that deter you from following God's commands to speak the truth.

TOUGH GUYS OFTEN STAND ALONE OR IN THE MINORITY

Majority rule is a democratic principle, not a biblical one. Just because the majority of people believe something doesn't make it morally right or OK. At different times in history, in different parts of the world, the majority of people have been openly racist. That didn't make it OK. As late as the 1970s, there were still laws in the U.S., passed by majorities in certain states, allowing the government to force some women to undergo sterilization.[30] The fact that a majority of lawmakers agreed with this horrific practice didn't make it OK. Today, in some states, there are majorities that believe the murder of unborn babies should continue to be legal. That doesn't somehow make it right.

When we find ourselves in the minority in a certain belief, it's easy to question ourselves. It's natural to doubt our convictions when so many other people disagree. However, when it comes to biblical truths that run counter to our culture, we must fight the urge to conform. The Tough Guys didn't conform. Even though they were often alone or at least in the minority, they held to their convictions. Gideon was in the minority when he knocked down the altar to Baal. At certain times, Jeremiah's only friend may have been his scribe Baruch. Daniel seemed to be alone when he challenged the

---

30. http://disabilityjustice.tpt.org/right-to-self-determination-freedom-from-involuntary-sterilization/

kings of Babylon. JTB continued to condemn King Herod even while he was a prisoner separated from his disciples.

In ancient times, speaking an unpopular truth might have gotten you killed. Today, in our country, it's much more common that Christians who speak difficult biblical truths are called names. We're called bigots or anti-this or that. Jesus warned this would happen and even called those who endure it, blessed.

> *Blessed are you when others revile you and persecute you and utter all kinds of evil against you falsely on my account. Rejoice and be glad, for your reward is great in heaven, for so they persecuted the prophets who were before you. (Matthew 5:11-12)*

The Tough Guys' examples show us that at times we will be called to stand alone in defense of God's commands. We must be willing to stand alone despite the lies and persecution. We should certainly push back on the lies by exposing the darkness and bringing the light of truth. Whether we're successful in persuading others or continue to receive insults, we must be willing to stand alone. Of course, we're never alone when God is on our side. The point is that we must be willing to stand alone among men, knowing that all things are in God's hands.

DON'T BE ASHAMED OF GOD'S COMMANDS

The Tough Guys weren't ashamed of God's commands; they proclaimed them and explained them. They didn't pick the commands of God they thought would be received well by each audience and focus on them; they spoke the truth boldly. In fact, they often focused specifically on the commands their audiences were ignoring. Many of the Apostle Paul's letters were to Christian churches, and he didn't hold back. He highlighted the areas where they were failing to live out the commands of the Bible. Paul wasn't ashamed of God's commands.

When JTB spoke to Herod, he didn't avoid God's commands about marriage because they might offend Herod who had married his brother's wife. JTB could have convinced himself that he should tell Herod about God's love and forgiveness and perhaps that would change the king's heart and eventually he would "see the light" on all those other tough issues like marriage. JTB could have talked about the easy parts of God's law and let someone else deal with the difficult areas. He didn't do that. JTB went right at Herod's sin. He wasn't ashamed of God's commands.

There are many politicians who claim to be Christians (and some who actually are). They often speak of their faith to appeal to voters who are Christians (or at least identify with Christianity). However, I hear very few of them pointing to God's commands when it's controversial to do so. In the current debate over marriage in our country, very few politicians who claim to be Christian will make the case that marriage should be between a man and a woman simply because that's God's command. They hide behind frameworks such as, *It should be a state's rights issue* or, *The voters should decide*. Critics will say we can't make laws based on religion, but that is completely ridiculous. Most of the laws of our country have their basis in the Mosaic Law that comes from the Bible. If we can't base our laws on religion, I guess we should get rid of those pesky laws against murder, stealing, and fraud.

MLK appealed to the commands of the Bible to make his case that segregation was wicked, wrong, and sinful. Was MLK wrong in how he challenged segregation? I dare you to post that online if you believe it. Even the Founding Fathers wrote in the Declaration of Independence that men had rights "endowed by their Creator."

What's even more incredible is that the people who want to change our laws away from the commands of the Bible have their own religion. They are atheists and secular humanists. Those are religions. They may not have their beliefs clearly written down (which by the way makes it very convenient when they want to change those beliefs, as they frequently do). The belief that their definition of marriage is the correct one is a truth statement, taken on faith. What makes them different from most politicians who claim to be Christians is that they are not ashamed of their religious beliefs. They're absolutely willing to promote their beliefs as "good" and "right." Quite frankly, the atheists and secular humanists have more conviction about what they believe than most politicians who claim to be Christians.

I would be remiss if I didn't point out that many politicians who claim to be Christian openly hold beliefs that are in opposition to God's commands. These "leaders" are very confused about what it means to be a Christian. They are only able to continue to call themselves Christians because too few actual Christians will call them out for their heretical beliefs.

Where are the Christian political leaders who are willing to defend their Christian beliefs in the public square simply because they are God's commands? Where are the Christian political leaders who aren't ashamed of God's commands? The Tough Guys weren't ashamed of God's commands.

As you look for examples of how to speak the truth of the Bible, you have many great examples in the Tough Guys.

COWARDS CAN'T CHANGE CULTURE

The Bible commands us to promote justice in our culture by exposing the evil of exploitation. Here are a few examples:

> *Open your mouth for the mute,*
> *for the rights of all who are destitute.*
> *Open your mouth, judge righteously,*
> *defend the rights of the poor and needy. (Proverbs 31:8-9)*
> *Take no part in the unfruitful works of darkness, but instead expose*
> *them. (Ephesians 5:11)*

Many churches today and in the past have been outspoken for justice. Christians have played a role in ending slavery, segregation, the burning alive of widows,[31] and infanticide, as well as providing for the poor. To accomplish this, Christians who lived before us had to speak up and say things that weren't popular in their day in order to change the culture. When William Wilberforce spoke out against slavery as a member of Parliament, it was not well received. He paid a price. Some believe he gave up his chance to be Prime Minister as a result of his uncompromising pursuit of justice. When Daniel challenged King Nebuchadnezzar to change his ways to attempt to avoid the judgment of his dream, he told him to end his sins and specifically identified his failure to show mercy to the oppressed as one of his sins.[liii] Some Bible translations use the word *poor* instead of *oppressed*. These men were speaking up to change the culture of their day.

One of the things I've observed at some churches is that they like the idea of promoting justice, but they aren't willing to be persecuted for it. They resolve this conflict by talking about justice issues that are already popular in our culture. Some churches will talk a lot about racial justice, ending sex trafficking, and taking care of the poor. To be sure, these are all important and worthy justice issues. Sadly, racism has not been defeated in our country. Sex trafficking is a wicked practice that is all too common, and Christians are clearly commanded to take care of the poor. However, our culture is completely in favor of those particular justice issues. Almost nobody would admit to being a racist, being in favor of sex trafficking, or being opposed to taking care of poor people. If you said any of those

---

31. If you're not familiar with the stories of Christians who worked to end the practice of Sati (burning widows alive), read this article: https://christianhistoryinstitute.org/magazine/article/ministry-in-killing-fields.

things out loud, you would be immediately ostracized by your friends and coworkers and possibly beaten up.

If you don't believe me, spend the next week addressing everyone you meet with racial slurs while you explain your plan to close down all homeless shelters and turn them into brothels filled exclusively with women who've been kidnapped and forced into prostitution. If, at the end of the week, you haven't been beaten up so many times that you're in a coma in a hospital under the name John Doe because nobody will admit they know you, send me an e-mail and tell me how that worked out for you. You can send it to youweretotallyright@iwillneverdoubtyouagain.com.

Christians are commanded to speak up for justice, but if you only focus on issues where the culture already agrees with you, by definition, you're not changing the culture. You're simply echoing the culture. You're preaching to the choir. You're reinforcing what everybody already believes. There is nothing wrong with joining the culture to speak up about popular justice issues, but it's not going to lead to much-needed cultural change. In addition, you should not kid yourself that somehow you're taking the same kind of risks that Wilberforce took when he challenged slavery, or MLK took when he challenged segregation. These men addressed these issues when they were unpopular and when it was difficult. It is because of their sacrifice that it's so *easy* for you to talk openly about these things today.

If you truly want to change the culture, you need to talk about the justice issues where the Bible and the culture come into conflict today. These are the truths that our culture needs to hear. They are not difficult to identify. In our country today, three obvious justice issues where the Bible and the culture come into conflict are abortion, the definition of marriage, and sexual immorality. Volumes of research have been published showing the harm in these areas when we as a culture ignore the commands of the Bible. There is plenty of ammunition available to show that truth is on the side of the Bible. However, it's difficult to talk about these issues today because the biblical view is unpopular. If you want to change the culture and promote justice, that's what's required. If you want to change the culture, by definition, you will initially be in the minority.

Many Christians want to believe that if they lived in the past, they would have spoken out against slavery, stood up against the Holocaust, or protested to end segregation. You don't have to wonder whether you would have had the courage to do those things. You simply have to ask yourself whether you're speaking out on the issues that are difficult today. The men who are speaking out on abortion, the definition of marriage, and sexual integrity today are the same men who would have spoken out against the past injustices of slavery, genocide, and segregation. The men who remain silent on the difficult issues today are the same men who would have remained silent in the past. I know many men who remain silent will disagree with this, but what evidence from their actions can they offer to the contrary?

What makes the Tough Guys so impressive is that they weren't cowards. They derived truth from the Bible (or the portion of the Scriptures that had been written when they lived). They exposed the darkness. They spoke up and many times changed the culture. When JTB spoke, many confessed their sins and were baptized.[liv] The Apostle Paul set up many new churches and helped Christianity spread rapidly. When we speak the truth boldly, it can change the culture.

YOUR WORDS REVEAL YOUR HEART

About twenty years ago, I had a moment of clarity about the love we have for celebrities in our country. Somebody was criticizing Weird Al Yankovic for his song parodies. Immediately, I jumped to his defense. I made a fairly compelling case that Weird Al's songs were harmless fun filled with clever observations and that he must be a humble guy because he predominantly mocked himself. Then it occurred to me. *Why I am I defending Weird Al? I don't even know Weird Al. I doubt Weird Al is defending me. This is an incredibly stupid use of my time, intellect, and energy.* I resolved to never waste another moment of my life defending a celebrity ever again.

Why do we get so offended when somebody criticizes a celebrity or sports figure we like? We don't even know these people. We will go to the mat to argue the case for why our sports hero is better than yours. Many a fight has started with a debate about sports teams. There are actually people who earn a living doing nothing but critiquing the lives of celebrities: what they wear, who they date, where they live. Why do we spend so much time talking about this as a culture? The answer is simple: We love our celebrities and sports heroes. We spend a lot of time talking about the things we love. We spend time talking about the things that are most important to us. Our words reveal our hearts.

The Tough Guys loved God. As a result, they used their words to explain and proclaim His commands. When I read about Jeremiah going to the temple, begging people to repent, I can feel the passion he had. He loved God and wanted the people to repent so badly. He didn't waste his breath on meaningless talk about things that would pass away. He focused on things that were eternal. Mark paints a picture of what it was like when JTB began his ministry:

> *And all the country of Judea and all Jerusalem were going out to him and were being baptized by him in the river Jordan, confessing their sins. (Mark 1:5)*

If the whole country was going out to him, he must have been saying the same thing over and over, day after day, so that they could all hear him. He must have been incredibly focused on the message of repentance.

When I read the Apostle Paul's letters and his passionate defense of God, it's so easy to see that his heart was focused on God. He didn't waste his words on meaningless debates. He got right to the point. His letter to the Romans might be the greatest letter ever written. It's jam-packed with insights and explanations of God's commands and the power of Jesus' crucifixion. His words revealed that his love and affection were for God. In Matthew, Jesus explained the importance of our words.

> *I tell you, on the day of judgment people will give account for every careless word they speak, for by your words you will be justified, and by your words you will be condemned. (Mathew 12:36-37)*

That is a scary thought. Our words reveal our hearts, and we will be held accountable for each one of them. Ask yourself whether your words reveal a love for God or whether your words reveal a greater love for something else.

IT'S NOT COMPASSIONATE TO REMAIN SILENT

When I read about the Tough Guys, one of the many things that impresses me is that they took the initiative in speaking the truth. They didn't wait until they were asked. They saw people who were lost in the lies of the world and proactively proclaimed truth. Daniel didn't wait for someone to ask his opinion when Nebuchadnezzar was going to kill all his wise men for failing to tell him his dream, he asked for a meeting with the king.[lv] Daniel could have just told Arioch, the king's captain, about the dream and had him relay the message, or he could have waited for someone to ask his opinion, but he didn't do that. He went straight to the source of darkness to give light to the dream that was causing so much trouble.

Acts describes the Apostle Paul's approach when he went to a new city.

TOUGH GUYS OF THE BIBLE

Now when they had passed through Amphipolis and Apollonia, they came to Thessalonica, where there was a synagogue of the Jews. And Paul went in, as was his custom, and on three Sabbath days he reasoned with them from the Scriptures, explaining and proving that it was necessary for the Christ to suffer and to rise from the dead, and saying, "This Jesus, whom I proclaim to you, is the Christ." (Acts 17:1-3)

The reason Paul went to the synagogue in each new city was because the religious and civic leaders were there. He wanted to take the gospel directly to the most prominent individuals of the city where his teaching would quickly spread across many social circles. Paul didn't set up a little booth at the edge of town and wait for people to come ask him questions. He went to the intellectual leaders of the city and reasoned with them. The Tough Guys brought light to the darkness by proclaiming truth where it needed to be heard.

If you could resurrect the Tough Guys and bring them to New York City and have them do exactly what they did in biblical times, many Christians would be horrified.[32] They would call the Tough Guys judgmental. They would say they lack grace. They would accuse them of failing to make the gospel relevant to the culture. They would probably be labeled crazy or legalistic. Christians would take them aside and try to educate them on how we "do church" in New York City and why they need to be more "seeker friendly." The good news is that the Tough Guys would completely ignore the advice of these Christians and continue to speak the truth boldly. That is because the Tough Guys had more compassion for men's souls than for their feelings.

There is an odd belief in many Christian communities that if you challenge people about their sin and call them to repent that you lack grace. If you buy into this point of view, then of all the men in the Bible, Jonah was probably the one most filled with grace. When God told him to go proclaim the coming judgment to the Ninevites because of their sin, he took a ship going the other direction.[lvi] He didn't want to go to Nineveh. He didn't want to call anyone a sinner. He wanted 120,000 people to be judged by God and perish since they were enemies of Israel.[lvii] The reality is that Jonah wasn't full of grace. He lacked compassion. He remained silent because he *didn't care* about the fate of the Ninevites.

While the Tough Guys would be labeled as uncaring by many Christians today, we know that they didn't speak the truth boldly because

32. While many Christians would be horrified, many others would be excited that men were speaking the truth so boldly.

they were just stubborn and insensitive about the impact of their words—the cost was way too high. Many were tortured, imprisoned, and killed as a result of the truth they proclaimed. Nobody would pay that price just because they enjoyed making people "feel judged." The Tough Guys spoke the truth out of an abundance of compassion. They cared enough that they were willing to be persecuted to get this truth out.

God has also made it clear that He doesn't want us to remain silent. Read His command to Ezekiel:

> *"So you, son of man, I have made a watchman for the house of Israel. Whenever you hear a word from my mouth, you shall give them warning from me. If I say to the wicked, O wicked one, you shall surely die, and you do not speak to warn the wicked to turn from his way, that wicked person shall die in his iniquity, but his blood I will require at your hand. But if you warn the wicked to turn from his way, and he does not turn from his way, that person shall die in his iniquity, but you will have delivered your soul."* (Ezekiel 33:7-9)

God made it clear that Ezekiel couldn't just remain silent. If he did, God would hold him accountable for the Israelites' failure to repent. This isn't limited to the Old Testament and Israel. Paul addressed this when he spoke to the Ephesian elders before going to Jerusalem.

> *Therefore I testify to you this day that I am innocent of the blood of all, for I did not shrink from declaring to you the whole counsel of God.* (Acts 20:26-27)

Paul declared his innocence because he spoke the truth directly. If he remained silent, he couldn't make that claim. Much like Ezekiel, there would have been blood on his hands. I think many Christians today fall into this trap of thinking it's somehow compassionate to remain silent. However, the cost of our silence could be eternal damnation for others. How is that compassionate? It's clearly not. If you're tempted to remain silent when you see those around you stuck in unrepentant sin, remember the Tough Guys and summon both the courage and compassion to speak up as they did.

THE TOUGH GUYS HAD DOUBTS

Despite their courage and perseverance, the Tough Guys sometimes had doubts. When God called him, Jeremiah initially protested that his youth made him unqualified.[lviii] The Creator of the universe had contacted

Jeremiah directly and given him an assignment. That kind of endorsement ought to inspire confidence in oneself, but Jeremiah responded with doubt. Later, he even tried to resign from his role as prophet but said God overpowered him.[lix] (Apparently, God does not accept resignation letters.) Since Jeremiah faced day after day of mocking and persecution from the people of his day, it's not surprising that he had doubts about his mission. While he occasionally griped to God about it, Jeremiah still continued his prophetic work.

Perhaps the most well-known story of Tough Guy doubt is when JTB was in jail. Even though he had earlier identified Jesus as the Son of God, JTB questioned whether He was in fact the Messiah.

> *Now when John heard in prison about the deeds of the Christ, he sent word by his disciples and said to him, "Are you the one who is to come, or shall we look for another?" And Jesus answered them, "Go and tell John what you hear and see: the blind receive their sight and the lame walk, lepers are cleansed and the deaf hear, and the dead are raised up, and the poor have good news preached to them. And blessed is the one who is not offended by me."*

> *Truly, I say to you, among those born of women there has arisen no one greater than John the Baptist. Yet the one who is least in the kingdom of heaven is greater than he. (Matthew 11:2-6, 11)*

John had dedicated his life to proclaiming the coming of the Messiah who he identified as Jesus. However, after he was put into prison, JTB questioned whether Jesus was really the Messiah. That's a *significant* detail. If Jesus wasn't the Messiah, then JTB had identified a regular man as the Son of God. That would have meant he baptized a fraudster—that's a pretty big doubt. Despite that, Jesus still said there was no one greater among men than JTB. God doesn't want us to doubt; but when we do, it doesn't disqualify us from leading or serving the kingdom. Jesus praised JTB even though he had doubts. Don't let your doubts hold you back from serving the kingdom. You should certainly wrestle with your doubts and resolve them through prayer and Scripture reading, but don't use doubt as an excuse to step back from serving God. The Tough Guys wrestled with their doubts, and God continued to use them.

SOMETIMES PEOPLE LISTEN, SOMETIMES THEY DON'T

One lesson we learn from the Tough Guys is that when you speak the truth, sometimes people listen . . . and sometimes they don't. Jeremiah spoke the truth, and nobody listened to him even though he was always right. If I could go back in time, I would bring Jeremiah a T-shirt that said, "I Told You So" in big bold letters on the front and "Believe Me Now or Believe Me Later" on the back. His lack of success had nothing to do with his level of faith or his persuasiveness. People were just not receptive. Other prophets in his day, including Ezekiel and Uriah the son of Shemaiah,[lx] were also unsuccessful in persuading Judah to repent and return to God. Jeremiah didn't fail. He was successful in following the commands of God. It was Judah who failed when they neglected to heed his warnings and repent.

JTB had some success. Many people in Judah responded to his call to repent and came out to be baptized by him, but Herod refused to repent of marrying his brother's wife even though JTB challenged him directly. The Apostle Paul had tremendous success persuading people to follow Jesus and setting up churches throughout the Roman world. However, he was constantly writing letters back to those churches, challenging them to live out what they believed. Many listened and believed but then forgot.

As Christian men speaking the truth, we can't judge our success by counting how many people seem to follow Jesus when we talk to them. We have to be obedient even if it doesn't appear that we're having success in the eyes of the world. Of course we should use the wisdom and talents God has given us to speak the truth in the most effective way, but we don't know God's larger plan. JTB seemed to have great success with all his followers, but it's unclear how many conversions were sincere. Jeremiah appeared to be a colossal failure as a prophet, but more than twenty-five hundred years later, we're still reading his writings. While his words may have fallen on deaf ears in his day, they have guided and blessed so many more after his death. It's doubtful that Jeremiah could have conceived of the impact he would have over thousands of years. How could he even imagine a world where his words would be translated into more than five hundred languages, and people would spend years writing commentaries on what he said? With the advent of the internet and the ease with which information is catalogued and shared today, we have no idea when our words will be used by God. Like the Tough Guys, we need to obediently speak the truth and let God leverage it for His purposes.

CHRISTIAN EXCUSES FOR NOT SPEAKING UP

This was one of the most fun sections of the book to write because it gave me an opportunity to mock people who say dumb things. You may be thinking, *It's sinful to mock people.* In that case, I mock you for failing to read the Bible closely. The wisest man who ever lived (other than Jesus) started

Proverbs by challenging his readers to heed wisdom and mocking those who didn't.

> *Because I have called and you refused to listen,*
> *have stretched out my hand and no one has heeded,*
> *because you have ignored all my counsel*
> *and would have none of my reproof,*
> *I also will laugh at your calamity;*
> *I will mock when terror strikes you,*
> *when terror strikes you like a storm*
> *and your calamity comes like a whirlwind,*
> *when distress and anguish come upon you.*
> *Then they will call upon me, but I will not answer;*
> *they will seek me diligently but will not find me.*
> *Because they hated knowledge*
> *and did not choose the fear of the Lord,*
> *would have none of my counsel*
> *and despised all my reproof,*
> *therefore they shall eat the fruit of their way,*
> *and have their fill of their own devices. (Proverbs 1:24-31)*

Solomon mocked people when terror struck them because they would not listen to wisdom. Following his lead, I'm going to mock people who demonstrate that they are refusing to listen to wisdom by saying really dumb things. Sadly, many people claiming to be Christians will use the most ridiculous excuses for failing to speak the truth directly. Very often, the reality is that they just want people to like them, so they refuse to talk about the challenging parts of the Bible. I'm going to list a series of excuses I've heard over the years and give examples of how you might respond. In some cases, I will translate what they said to demonstrate how silly it is and then show you how to challenge them to be more like the Tough Guys.

I want to be strategic in how we approach that subject.

Translation: *I have no intention of addressing this biblical truth, but I'm hoping that if I use a big word, like strategic, you will be so intimidated by my intellect that you won't push the topic any further and we'll move on to something else. My strategy is to avoid the topic and hope that someone else addresses it. If the tide turns and the culture starts to agree with that biblical truth, I'll be right behind all of you.*

Whenever you hear a Christian man say this, make a simple request: "So tell me your strategy." Then watch as he struggles to formulate a strategy on the spot that makes some rational sense. I've had men who've been in ministry for years say this to me. If you've been a Christian for five years, ten years, fifteen years, or more, and you still haven't formulated a strategy for challenging other men on difficult biblical truths, what are you waiting for? Does it take twenty years to create a strategy? JTB only ministered for about three years and he figured it out. The Tough Guys had a very simple strategy. They challenged men who ignored the commands of God. You need to adopt a similar strategy.

Jesus was a peacemaker.

Translation: *I prefer to ignore the parts of the Bible where Jesus talked about judgment, turned over the tables in the temple, and angered people so much that they executed him. I can't really reconcile how a peacemaker specifically said He didn't come to bring peace but rather came with a sword to set a man against his father, but I'll just keep saying Jesus was a peacemaker and hope that the conversation goes in a different direction.* [lxi]

If someone says this to you, simply ask him, "If Jesus was such a peacemaker, why exactly did they execute him?" Loving your neighbor as yourself does not mean only telling him what he wants to hear. Speaking truth creates tension. The Tough Guys understood this.

If I talk about the controversial parts of the Bible, people won't come back to church, and I'll lose the opportunity to tell them about Jesus.

Translation: *I would rather have a big church full of people who don't believe the truth of the Bible than a little church full of people who do.*

If someone says this to you, ask him, "What Jesus are you going to tell them about?" The story of Jesus is offensive to our culture. If you don't talk about the controversial parts of the Bible, you're not talking about the real Jesus.

Christians shouldn't be against anything.

Translation: *Christians shouldn't be against anything that our culture likes.*

This is a fairly simple one. Just ask, "Are you against slavery? Are you against stealing? Are you against punching little old ladies in the stomach?" Then watch him squirm. Of course Christians should be against things. Christians have played a role in bringing about justice many times throughout history precisely because they were against those injustices and were willing to speak up and endure persecution to help bring them to an end. The Tough Guys spoke against a lot of things. Can you imagine if Elijah said to God, "I don't want to be against Ahab's idol worship. Can't I just talk about how great You are and hope he figures out he shouldn't be worshiping Baal?" This is a silly excuse. Make sure you're prepared to mock any Christian man who tries to pass this off as an intelligent thought.

Focus on the major parts of the Bible.

Translation: *If it's popular, it's a major. If it's not popular, it's a minor.*

You should ask the speaker, "Who decides which are the important parts of the Bible and which are the parts we can minimize?" This is particularly offensive because the speaker is putting himself in the place of God. He is saying everyone should conform to his views of what is really important in the Bible.

God doesn't waste words. He is not known for being loquacious. If He put something in the Bible, it's there for a reason. In Isaiah, God even said His word shall not return to Him empty.[lxii] Don't fall for the lie that we can minimize something in the Bible and ignore it because it gets in the way of getting people in our culture to like us. There are no major and minor truths. Things are either true or not true. If they're not true, you can ignore them, and if they are true, you can't.

When King David and the men of Israel brought the Ark of the Covenant to Jerusalem, they made what many might consider a minor mistake. God had commanded the Israelites to transport the Ark of the Covenant on the shoulders of men using poles. In addition, God said that no man should touch the Ark or he would die.[lxiii] Despite this, the men of Israel chose to move it to Jerusalem using an ox cart. When the ox stumbled, Uzzah put his hand on the Ark to steady it, and God killed him.[lxiv] It seems harsh. Wasn't Uzzah just trying to prevent the Ark from falling? The men of Israel thought God's commands for handling the Ark were minors. Turns out that God thought they were majors. He cleared that up pretty quickly. God's commands are never minor. Don't trust the flawed wisdom of men when the clear and true commands of God are right in front of you in the Bible.

I don't want to get political.

Translation: *I don't want to take a position on anything that might cause somebody not to like me. I don't want to stand up for the defenseless because I might offend someone. I don't want to speak out for righteousness because there might be a cost to me economically or socially.*

When a man says this, he typically means he doesn't want to say anything controversial. The way to challenge him is to point out all the things he is willing to talk about that are political. Sex trafficking is political. Christian organizations are trying to pass laws all around the world aimed at protecting women. They are using a political process to try to promote justice for these women. Poverty is political. There is a huge debate in our country about the best way to use government resources to tackle poverty. This doesn't stop Christians from fighting poverty. The Tough Guys were incredibly political.

Moses was political when he went to Pharaoh and said, "Let my people go." John the Baptist was political when he challenged Herod, the king, for his unrighteous behavior. Jeremiah was political when he challenged the king of Israel to turn back to God. Elijah was political when he challenged Ahab and all the prophets of Baal. Who did all these men challenge? The political leaders of their day.

Many Christian men throughout history used the political process to promote justice. Wilberforce was political when he kept introducing laws in Parliament to end the slave trade. Dietrich Bonhoeffer was political when he stood up to the German church as they caved to Hitler. MLK was political when he participated in civil disobedience to end segregation. We admire these men because, through the lens of history, it's clear that they were on the side of morality and righteousness, but it wasn't that obvious in their time. They were all considered "political."

In fact, MLK wrote his letter from a Birmingham jail in response to eight religious leaders who wrote an open letter on April 12, 1963, titled "A Call for Unity."[33] They discouraged the local citizens from participating in the demonstrations, calling them "unwise and untimely." While they condemned hatred, they encouraged the local citizens to press their case

---

33.   http://www.newseum.org/education/teacher-resources/lesson-plans/the-first-amendment-and-social-change--mlk-s-letter-from-birmingham-jail-pdf.pdf

for rights in the courts and to negotiate with local leaders. *Really?* One hundred years after the Emancipation Proclamation, these leaders thought African Americans should just look to the courts and wait patiently? That wasn't a realistic strategy to achieve justice. It was a weak attempt to avoid controversy. They ended the letter by encouraging the citizens to "observe the principles of law and order and common sense." *Common sense?* Isn't it common sense that we shouldn't discriminate against people based on the color of their skin? Isn't it common sense to religious leaders that God made us all in His image?

Do you know any of the names of these eight religious leaders? *Of course not!* At a time when they should have had the courage to speak up for the oppressed, they chose instead to discourage people from getting "political." Don't fall for this. Tough guys speak up when there is injustice.

The history of slavery provides us with a clear model of how to deal with "political" situations. Never has there been a more political issue in our country. It divided the country and brought on a war that to this day had more casualties than all other U.S. wars combined. There were three beliefs about slavery in early America: There were those who said it was always wrong. There were those who said it was always OK. Then there were those who said it was OK some of the time. These were the "reasonable" people of their day. They were in the "middle," so they were able to see both sides. They weren't like those crazy "extremists" who said something was "always right" or "always wrong."

History has taught us that the people who said slavery should always be illegal were absolutely correct. The people who said slavery should always be legal were absolutely wrong. And the people who said slavery should be legal in some cases and illegal in others were also *absolutely wrong, but in addition to being wrong, they were spineless.* While some may seem reasonable today for seeing "both sides" and not getting "political," if they're on the wrong side of God's righteousness, in the end, they will always be absolutely wrong.

The idea that Christians shouldn't get political is a lie from Satan. You will not find that command in the Bible because it isn't there. If Christians don't speak up on these controversial topics, then the only voices in the public square will be those who oppose God. What an amazing trick by Satan. He has convinced the Christians to silence themselves so that those who hate Jesus can influence the culture with their lies without any competition from men speaking the truth. As I've already outlined, Christians are commanded by God to speak up and are blessed when they are persecuted for defending Jesus.

There are churches where the ministers will speak with great affection about Wilberforce, Bonhoeffer, and MLK, and highlight their courage. However, when you suggest to them that the church engage in similar activities today to challenge the unrighteousness of our culture such as abortion, redefining marriage, or sexual immorality, they recoil and tell you not to be "political."

It can be challenging for a minister to take these things on since his congregation might leave. It's always easy for you, as a congregant, to complain that the minister isn't speaking up enough. If the church has financial difficulty, that doesn't hurt you. You can just go to another church. So if you need to challenge your minister, do it gently and in a spirit of encouragement. There are a couple of steps you need to take.

First, live it. You need to be willing to speak up about these issues and take on the risk you're asking others to bear. Second, take the time to encourage your ministers and make a commitment to them. Make sure they know you will stick by them if they speak openly on these tough issues. If it hurts the church, you can't bail. You have to stick around and help the church through the challenging times. Third, you have to challenge other men in the church to "live it" on these issues and commit to supporting the church leadership. Unless you plan to pay the minister's salary all by yourself when everyone else leaves because the elders speak directly, you need to challenge other men to commit to the church and not leave if things get tough. Fourth, you have to open yourself up to being challenged. If you're trying to change people's minds, make sure you're listening to what they say and not just talking "at" them. Proverbs says, "As iron sharpens iron, so one person sharpens another."[lxv] Finally, you have to pray all the time. Ask God for wisdom in how to deal with these issues in a productive way that's not divisive. You can be challenging without being nasty. You're there to change people's minds and turn them to righteousness, not zing them because they're not living up to your standards. The Tough Guys were firm but humble, knowing that the truth they spoke was not of themselves but of God. Do everything in a spirit of encouragement and not anger.

It has really been a blast to write this section. I could go on for many more pages, but my mother said I'm starting to sound obnoxious.[34] As you face difficult decisions about when and how to speak about difficult biblical truths, look to the Tough Guys for guidance and encouragement.

---

34. She always says that though, so maybe it's just a reflex at this point in my life.

Chapter 11

PASTOR'S LOG: SAVING CHURCHES AND SOULS

TOM: CHALLENGING MEN ON THEIR ATTITUDES

When I first arrived at Christ Community Church, I met Tom,[35] a blacksmith who lived a quiet life dominated by hard work and service to others. He worked at an oil company building the tools that workers needed in their jobs at the refinery. Everyone there knew Tom as a hard worker. An elder at the church, he volunteered a lot of his time managing the building. One summer, he and a group of other men dug out a basement for the church by hand so that there would be a place for the congregation to have events. I doubt many churches today could convince a group of men to volunteer that much time to work on a project that dirty and unpleasant, but Tom didn't have to be asked; he offered. Many dinners, Sunday school classes, and wedding receptions took place in that basement. It continued as a valuable resource for the church for many years. When Tom retired, he took a portion of his retirement savings and spent a year on the mission field in Zimbabwe (then called Rhodesia) with his adult son. He spent his life serving quietly.

---

35. Pseudonym used to protect the individual's identity.

Even facing death, Tom thought about others. When he received a cancer diagnosis, he asked that people would pray for him to die with a good testimony. He wanted to be a great example to other Christians even in the way he died. He didn't want to become angry or bitter for the suffering he would endure but rather show thankfulness for all that God had given him. He epitomized true servanthood until the very end of his life.

People who knew Tom said of him, "What you see is what you get." He didn't have any hidden agendas; he made his intentions clear. Tom also told you what he thought. He didn't talk about you behind your back or silently judge you; he spoke the truth directly. When one of his sons got his girlfriend pregnant and had a quick marriage, Tom had a direct conversation with his new daughter-in-law. He said, "We don't like the way you came into the family, but we will love you as best we can." She respected him ever since and built such a strong relationship with him over the years that she was inconsolable when he died.

As a result of Tom's servant attitude toward life, he had the opportunity to speak the truth directly without alienating people. His actions demonstrated a selfless agenda. He chose to serve others rather than himself. This allowed Tom to challenge men in a productive way. Prior to my arrival as a new pastor, there was serious tension at the church. Some of the members disagreed on the future direction and many thought it inevitable that the church would split. The elders asked Tom to take over as the chair of the board and bring unity to the church. Tom's reputation for straight talk and selfless service made him the perfect man for the job. He had direct conversations with some men and told them their attitudes were creating tension. He challenged them on their words and interactions with others. He reminded them that the church hadn't had splits in the past and didn't need to have them in the future. He brought unity to the church leadership by challenging the men to stop complaining. He spoke directly to the issues and brought about resolutions. His pure motives, reputation for service, and clear language allowed him to lead without upsetting people.

God used Tom to save a church and demonstrate Christian leadership. His story, known to only a few, is a great example of Tough Guy leadership. He served for God's glory rather than his own. He led first by example. He spoke the truth directly when it could have cost him relationships. He took risks even though he had nothing to gain. His life was a testament to serving others rather than yourself and volunteering your gifts for the kingdom of God.

JONATHAN EDWARDS: TELLING SINNERS THE TRUTH THEY NEEDED TO HEAR

Jonathan Edwards, a well-known pastor from Northampton, Massachusetts, lived in the 1700s. He played a significant role in the First Great Awakening when many people in the American Colonies became Christians. His sermons and writing still influence many today, especially Christians in Reformed denominations. Edwards knew how to speak the truth directly. While he wrote clear and direct sermons, he spoke at a level pitch. He was not known to shout at his congregation but rather delivered his messages in a firm but quiet voice. He conveyed difficult truths with deep biblical exegesis rather than worldly emotion.

One of his most famous sermons was titled, "Sinners in the Hands of an Angry God." The first time I read the sermon, I was struck by how many times he used the words *hell*, *sin*, *fire*, and *wrath*. The table below lists the number of times he used each word:

Hell	51
Sin/sinners	17
Wrath	52
Fire	17

There are churches in our country where you might not hear the word *hell* from the pulpit fifty-one times in an entire year. You might not even hear it fifty-one times in five years. There is a fear of being labeled a "fire and brimstone" preacher who is trying to scare his congregation into repentance. If you preached Edwards' sermon today, you might be labeled as judgmental or lacking grace. However, Edwards used this sermon very effectively to challenge his listeners to turn back to God. His direct language, including sermons such as this, played a role in bringing about a Great Awakening where many people gave their lives to Jesus. Isn't that the goal? Aren't we trying to tell people the truth about heaven and hell so that they understand the eternal significance of their choices and join us in proclaiming Jesus as Lord and Savior? Clearly, we are.

Edwards is quoted frequently by pastors today because of his powerful insight into the Bible. He studied the Bible for up to thirteen hours a day. His writings are incredibly insightful and continue to enlighten Christians today. While his greatest impact to Christianity has probably come after his death through his writings, Edwards was a Tough Guy in his day because he spoke the truth directly. He didn't scream or shout to get you to believe.

He simply told his listeners the facts of what the Bible says. He told people what they needed to hear about the reality of heaven, hell, and a God who literally became human to die for us. God used Edwards' direct language, both in person and in written form, to open the eyes of many. Most of us will never have his intellect or the discipline to study the Bible the way he did, but we can all model his approach to speaking the truth directly.[lxvi]

Chapter 12

JESUS SPOKE THE TRUTH DIRECTLY TO MAKE DISCIPLES

There are many leaders in business, government, and churches who only want to deliver positive messages to their employees, constituents, or congregants. They will delegate difficult conversations to their subordinates. They show up for all the ribbon cutting ceremonies and positive announcements while they conveniently take vacation on the days when their organizations announce a layoff. Jesus was not that kind of leader. He delivered difficult messages Himself. He directly addressed the controversies of His day. Jesus rebuked and challenged both friends and foes not out of anger or spite but out of love and a sincere hope they would repent and choose light over darkness.

Jesus led by speaking the truth directly. Let's start with one of the many passages where Jesus talked about judgment.

> *Then he began to denounce the cities where most of his mighty works had been done, because they did not repent. "Woe to you, Chorazin! Woe to you, Bethsaida! For if the mighty works done in you had been done in Tyre and Sidon, they would have repented long ago in sackcloth and ashes. But I tell you, it will be more bearable on the day of judgment for Tyre and Sidon than for you. And you, Capernaum, will you be exalted to heaven? You will be brought down to Hades. For if the mighty works done in you had*

been done in Sodom, it would have remained until this day. But I
tell you that it will be more tolerable on the day of judgment for the
land of Sodom than for you." (Matthew 11:20-24)

Sodom and Gomorrah were the biblical poster children for bad behavior. The people of those cities sinned against God so severely that He killed everyone with fire from heaven.[lxvii] If your city's judgment is going to be worse than Sodom's, you are in for some serious pain and suffering. Jesus' message here is direct: judgment awaits if you don't repent.

Some Christians seem to think Jesus was God's hippie alter ego who only spoke of peace and harmony. Maybe they think after all the war and judgment in the Old Testament, God took a four-hundred-year vacation on a beach in some galaxy we don't even know about and came back as a Bohemian with some *really far out insight into mankind.* I often wonder if I am reading the same Bible as these Christians. Did we discover some scroll that proves that the ancient Greek words for *hell* and *judgment* have been mistranslated for over two thousand years and really have meant "paradise" and "forgiveness" all along? Of course not! God is unchanging. He spoke of both love and judgment in the Old Testament, and Jesus spoke of both love and judgment in the New Testament.

Jesus taught His disciples to love their enemies, but that didn't stop Him from challenging the Pharisees.[lxviii] He called them some pretty unpleasant things.

"Woe to you, scribes and Pharisees, hypocrites! For you clean the outside of the cup and the plate, but inside they are full of greed and self-indulgence. You blind Pharisee! First clean the inside of the cup and the plate, that the outside also may be clean.

"Woe to you, scribes and Pharisees, hypocrites! For you are like whitewashed tombs, which outwardly appear beautiful, but within are full of dead people's bones and all uncleanness. So you also outwardly appear righteous to others, but within you are full of hypocrisy and lawlessness.

"Woe to you, scribes and Pharisees, hypocrites! For you build the tombs of the prophets and decorate the monuments of the righteous, saying, 'If we had lived in the days of our fathers, we would not have taken part with them in shedding the blood of the prophets.' Thus you witness against yourselves that you are sons of those who murdered the prophets. Fill up, then, the measure of your fathers.

You serpents, you brood of vipers, how are you to escape being sentenced to hell?" (Matthew 23:25-33)

In just eight verses, Jesus managed to call the Pharisees hypocrites, greedy, self-indulgent, blind, whitewashed tombs, lawless, sons of murderers, and snakes—not just one snake, a whole family of them. To quote Yosemite Sam, "Dem's fightin' words."[36] Anyone who thinks Jesus only spoke of peace and harmony clearly hasn't read the Bible very closely. Jesus took the Pharisees on and called them out for their unrighteousness. He not only called out the religious leaders but also went out of His way to rebuke them. He even challenged them on their thoughts.

And getting into a boat he crossed over and came to his own city. And behold, some people brought to him a paralytic, lying on a bed. And when Jesus saw their faith, he said to the paralytic, "Take heart, my son; your sins are forgiven." And behold, some of the scribes said to themselves, "This man is blaspheming." But Jesus, knowing their thoughts, said, "Why do you think evil in your hearts?" (Matthew 9:1-4)

Older men will often caution you to "pick your battles." That's generally good advice. In this case, Jesus could have easily let this situation pass without addressing it. After all, these scribes said this to themselves, not out loud. He didn't have to bring it up, but He did. Jesus chose *directness over diplomacy.* He wanted repentance from the people rather than praise for Himself. He loved these men so much that He told them what they needed to hear rather than what they wanted to hear.

Jesus didn't reserve His aggressive language for those who opposed Him, He also used it with His friends. When Peter rebuked Jesus and insisted that the religious leaders would not torture and kill Him, Jesus said, "Get behind me, Satan!"[lxix] Jesus called Peter "Satan." Satan is the most evil, horrible thing in the universe. Peter must have recoiled when Jesus called him Beelzebub, but Jesus used this language to make a point. He obviously loved Peter and went on to forgive him despite Peter's denials of him. Jesus didn't use direct language to offend but rather to challenge, teach, and exhort. He wasn't trying to wound Peter's ego; He was trying to teach him.

Jesus continued this lesson to His disciples by telling them if they wanted to follow Him, they had to take up a cross.[lxx] A cross in those days symbolized shame and punishment. Jesus painted an unappealing picture

---

36. *High Diving Hare*, 1949. http://www.imdb.com/character/ch0000588/quotes. Are you impressed that I found a reference for that? You should be.

of what it meant to be His follower; He didn't sugarcoat the reality. He made it clear that following Him meant shame and persecution from the culture. He told His disciples that the world hated Him because He called their works evil. Who wants to follow a leader whom everyone hates? Telling potential disciples that most people will revile you is not an effective recruiting strategy. Jesus didn't say this because He thought it would attract more followers; He said it because it was true. He wanted His followers to understand the difficult path they were choosing.

While Jesus came to save us from the consequences of our sins, He managed to alienate many people with His direct language. His conversation with the rich young ruler was astonishing.

> And as he was setting out on his journey, a man ran up and knelt before him and asked him, "Good Teacher, what must I do to inherit eternal life?" And Jesus said to him, "Why do you call me good? No one is good except God alone. You know the commandments: 'Do not murder, Do not commit adultery, Do not steal, Do not bear false witness, Do not defraud, Honor your father and mother.'" And he said to him, "Teacher, all these I have kept from my youth." And Jesus, looking at him, loved him, and said to him, "You lack one thing: go, sell all that you have and give to the poor, and you will have treasure in heaven; and come, follow me." Disheartened by the saying, he went away sorrowful, for he had great possessions. (Mark 10:17-22)

Rather than lower the standard for eternal life in the hope that the rich man would follow Him, Jesus seemed to raise the standard. To be clear, Jesus was not saying that everyone should sell his or her possessions to inherit eternal life. He recognized that the rich man idolized wealth and made it clear he needed to part with his idols in order to follow Jesus. The story is astonishing because so many ministries today view a rich man as someone who can help fund their mission. I have served on a few charity boards, and we were always trying to convince rich people that they should join our mission by donating to our organization. If I started alienating rich guys, I would probably have been kicked off the boards pretty quickly. But Jesus didn't need money from the rich man; He knew God would provide whatever He needed. Rather than think about what the rich man could do for His ministry, Jesus focused on what He could do for the rich man. He knew this man needed to be challenged on his idols even though it meant the man probably wouldn't support Jesus' ministry. That is bold and loving all at the same time.

One of my favorite chapters in the Bible is John 6 because it highlights the boldness of Jesus and the fickleness of people. Many people had just witnessed Jesus heal the sick and feed five thousand men (plus women and children), so they wanted to make Him the king. Jesus withdrew to the other side of the Sea of Galilee to avoid this, but many people pursued Him. When they caught up with Him, Jesus explained what it meant to follow Him.

> *"I am the living bread that came down from heaven. If anyone eats of this bread, he will live forever. And the bread that I will give for the life of the world is my flesh." The Jews then disputed among themselves, saying, "How can this man give us his flesh to eat?" So Jesus said to them, "Truly, truly, I say to you, unless you eat the flesh of the Son of Man and drink his blood, you have no life in you. Whoever feeds on my flesh and drinks my blood has eternal life, and I will raise him up on the last day. For my flesh is true food, and my blood is true drink. Whoever feeds on my flesh and drinks my blood abides in me, and I in him. As the living Father sent me, and I live because of the Father, so whoever feeds on me, he also will live because of me. This is the bread that came down from heaven, not like the bread the fathers ate, and died. Whoever feeds on this bread will live forever." Jesus said these things in the synagogue, as he taught at Capernaum.*
>
> *When many of his disciples heard it, they said, "This is a hard saying; who can listen to it?" But Jesus, knowing in himself that his disciples were grumbling about this, said to them, "Do you take offense at this? Then what if you were to see the Son of Man ascending to where he was before? It is the Spirit who gives life; the flesh is no help at all. The words that I have spoken to you are spirit and life. But there are some of you who do not believe." (For Jesus knew from the beginning who those were who did not believe, and who it was who would betray him.) And he said, "This is why I told you that no one can come to me unless it is granted him by the Father." After this many of his disciples turned back and no longer walked with him. (John 6:51-66)*

If I had to summarize this chapter in current vernacular, it would go something like this:

People: Jesus, You're awesome! You should be king.

Jesus: You have to eat my body and drink my blood to get into heaven.

People: Say what?

Jesus: You heard me!

People: We're outta here. This Hebrew's crazy!

They literally went from wanting to make Him king to completely abandoning Him in about twenty-four hours. Why did this happen? Because Jesus spoke the truth directly, and the people didn't like what they heard. What I love about this chapter is that Jesus didn't soften His language. He wasn't worried about attracting the most followers. Instead, He wanted sincere followers even if that meant there were a lot fewer of them. How many churches take that approach? How many churches are willing to risk alienating people by telling them the difficult truths? How many churches conform to the approach of Jesus?

What's even more shocking about this story is that Jesus didn't even try to explain it to them. When the people left, He could have called after them and said, "Come back. It was just a metaphor. You don't have to actually become cannibals. Let me use language that is more culturally acceptable to you. Let's just talk about the parts of the Scriptures that fit your current worldview. We'll deal with eating my body and drinking my blood later." Jesus didn't say that. He clearly wanted disciples who would follow Him even when His commands seemed weird and offensive. He wasn't willing to accept those who liked all His popular blessings (healing and feeding people) but rejected His unpopular commands (eating His body and drinking His blood).

Jesus went even further. After many of His followers left, He asked His twelve disciples, "Do you want to go away as well?"[lxxi] Jesus didn't thank them for sticking around. He didn't say, "Hey guys, I really appreciate your sticking by Me in this tough time when so many others are abandoning Me. You're real pals." No, instead He basically invited them to leave as well. Jesus did not speak in euphemisms. He didn't soften His language or focus on the popular things; Jesus spoke the truth directly even when it cost Him followers. That's bold! We should all go and do likewise.

PART IV
THEY EXCELLED AT WHAT THEY DID

Chapter 13

JOSEPH: FROM PRISON TO PRIME MINISTER

1898 BC	**Joseph** Sold into Slavery

BACKGROUND ON JOSEPH

God made a covenant with Abraham that He would bless his descendants. God fulfilled this promise through Abraham's son Isaac and through Isaac's son Jacob, whom God would later name Israel. Jacob had twelve sons who became the twelve tribes of Israel. Joseph was Jacob's eleventh son, and his older brothers didn't like him. There were three reasons for this. First, he told his father, Jacob, that his older brothers were doing a bad job taking care of the sheep. (Yes, he was a tattletale. This is not a Tough Guy quality, but he grew out of it.) Second, he had a dream that all of his brothers would one day bow down to him. (Here's a bit of advice to younger brothers everywhere: if you have a prophetic dream that your older brothers are going to bow down to you, keep it to yourself until you're big enough that they can't beat you up . . . because they will.) Finally, Jacob loved Joseph more than his other sons. I suppose it's hard not to have favorites when you have twelve boys, but this created a lot of problems.

Since his brothers hated him, they planned to kill him. (This is a fairly harsh penalty for being a tattletale, but as an older brother, I understand.

I'm not saying it's OK, but I get it.) Joseph's oldest brother, Reuben, convinced his brothers not to kill Joseph, but they eventually sold him into slavery to Midianite traders. For my brother's sake, it's a good thing this was not an option when I was growing up. Who wouldn't want to fix a tattletale problem and earn a profit at the same time? That's called a win-win situation. Unless of course you're the younger brother, in which case it's really a big lose situation.

Joseph was taken to Egypt at age seventeen and sold to a man named Potiphar, the captain of Pharaoh's bodyguards. Later, Potiphar's wife tried to seduce Joseph, but he repeatedly refused her. She eventually falsely accused him of trying to rape her, and Potiphar had Joseph thrown in jail.

Later, Pharaoh's cupbearer and chief baker were thrown into the same jail. They both had dreams that Joseph correctly interpreted for them. Pharaoh restored the cupbearer to his position in three days but hanged the chief baker just as Joseph had said. Two years later, after Pharaoh had two dreams that no one could interpret, the cupbearer suggested that Pharaoh call Joseph out of prison. The cupbearer was not a particularly thankful guy since it took him two years to remember what Joseph had done for him. If you're ever in prison and interpret someone's dream, don't hold your breath for a thank-you card.

Joseph explained to Pharaoh that his dreams meant there would be seven years of abundance in the land followed by seven years of famine. Joseph recommended Pharaoh store one-fifth of the harvest each year during the seven abundant years so there would be food during the famine. Pharaoh was so impressed that he put Joseph in charge of all of Egypt, only second in command to himself; he essentially made him Prime Minister. Joseph was thirty when this happened. How does a thirty-year-old foreign slave, in prison for attempted rape, become Prime Minister of probably the most powerful nation of his time? This could only be the hand of God.

When the seven years of famine came, Jacob sent his sons to Egypt to buy food. The brothers were brought before Joseph but didn't recognize him. They bowed down to him as he had dreamt years earlier. At first, Joseph challenged them and made them jump through hoops. You can't really blame him for that. What younger brother wouldn't love the opportunity to make his older brothers do whatever he says? But Joseph didn't take revenge. Instead he brought his father, Jacob, and all his brothers and their families down to Egypt and provided for them. The former tattletale grew into a courageous man who followed God faithfully and helped save many people from starvation.

HOW JOSEPH EXCELLED AT WHAT HE DID

The Bible says that God was with Joseph. As a result, he excelled at his work even at a young age. While only seventeen years old when sold into Potiphar's house, he performed so well in his duties that Potiphar put him in charge of his entire household. The household flourished, and Potiphar didn't have to concern himself with anything but what he ate.[lxxii] It was extraordinary that Potiphar not only entrusted someone so young but also someone who was a foreign slave. Joseph must have inspired incredible confidence with his management of the household, including his fields and crops. Since Potiphar had an important role in Egypt, he likely had a large estate, so this wasn't a small job for Joseph.

In jail, Joseph was so effective and trustworthy that the warden put him in charge of all the prisoners. Who puts a prisoner in charge of the jail? *Seriously?* Who does that? Joseph must have been very persuasive and effective. The Bible says, "The keeper of the prison paid no attention to anything that was in Joseph's charge because the Lord was with him. And whatever he did, the Lord made it succeed."[lxxiii] Joseph excelled in the most unlikely place.

Joseph also excelled in interpreting dreams. The baker and the cupbearer could not interpret their own dreams, but Joseph correctly showed them their meaning. Later, Joseph correctly interpreted Pharaoh's dream. Joseph must have been convincing since Pharaoh took Joseph from prisoner to second in command of Egypt just based on the interpretation.

Once in charge of Egypt, Joseph excelled in preparing the country for the coming famine. He went through the cities and set up storehouses. This allowed him to provide for Egypt but also have additional food available for foreigners. When the famine came, Joseph was able to sell food to both Egyptians and foreigners, which allowed Pharaoh to acquire even greater wealth.

> *Now there was no food in all the land, for the famine was very severe, so that the land of Egypt and the land of Canaan languished by reason of the famine. And Joseph gathered up all the money that was found in the land of Egypt and in the land of Canaan, in exchange for the grain that they bought. And Joseph brought the money into Pharaoh's house. (Genesis 47:13-14)*

Joseph essentially sold the Egyptians back their own grain which he had taken from them, thus launching the era of big government. We'll forgive him for this because God was with him.

As the famine continued, Joseph sold the grain and acquired all the Egyptians' livestock and land for Pharaoh. He then gave the Egyptians seed to plant on what was now Pharaoh's land and required that they give one-fifth to Pharaoh (landlords are brutal). He allowed them to keep four-fifths to feed themselves. While he acquired greater wealth for Pharaoh, he set up an economic system where the people would have an incentive to work hard on their land while creating ongoing income for Pharaoh.

Joseph excelled in everything he did because God was with him.

Chapter 14

NEHEMIAH: LEADING BY EXAMPLE

444 BC	**Nehemiah** Went to Jerusalem to Rebuild the Wall

BACKGROUND ON NEHEMIAH

About sixty-seven years after Nebuchadnezzar first took Daniel and others from Judah into captivity, the Persian King Cyrus conquered Babylon and allowed the Israelites to return to their homeland.[37] Some Israelites returned under the leadership of Zerubbabel (try saying that quickly three times in a row) and rebuilt the temple,[38] but other Israelites remained in Babylon or other parts of the Persian Empire.

More than ninety years after Zerubbabel (Zerubbabel, Zerubbabel, Zerubbbb . . .) returned, the walls of Jerusalem still had not been rebuilt, and the surrounding people were threatening the Israelites. Nehemiah was a Jew serving in a prominent position as cupbearer to King Artaxerxes of Persia. When Nehemiah heard about the state of Jerusalem, he was so upset that he asked the king if he could go to Jerusalem and rebuild the city.

---

37. In Jeremiah 25:8-14, he prophesied that Judah and other nations would serve Babylon for seventy years. While the captivity of Judah appears to be only sixty-seven years, the period of time from when Babylon first defeats the Assyrians (609 BC) to when they are defeated by the Persians (539 BC) fulfills the seventy-year prophesy.

38. The book of Ezra covers this period.

When Nehemiah arrived, he organized the people of Jerusalem to rebuild the wall. The surrounding people did not want the Israelites to gain the security of a walled city, so they opposed the efforts. At first they mocked them but then tried to fight them to prevent reconstruction. To protect against attack, Nehemiah set up guards for the city day and night. He also had the workers keep their weapons with them. In addition, Nehemiah instructed the leaders in each part of the city to blow a trumpet if they were attacked, and then the Israelites from the other parts of the city would come to their aid to fight off the invaders. Throughout this time, Nehemiah encouraged the people, who were scared, by reminding them that God was with them.

Nehemiah was able to rebuild the walls and the gates of Jerusalem in only fifty-two days. (Imagine if our government could work that efficiently.) Israel's enemies lost confidence and gave up the fight against them. Then Nehemiah reorganized the city and rebuilt the houses inside the walls. He had Ezra read the law to the people and call them to repentance. He challenged his fellow Israelites who were extracting usury (fancy word for high interest rates—loan shark high) from their brothers and selling them into slavery during a famine. He also challenged them for marrying foreign wives against God's command. Nehemiah was successful in challenging Judah. The leaders agreed to reform their culture and signed a covenant to keep God's laws.

Nehemiah governed Judah for twelve years and then returned briefly to work for King Artaxerxes. During that time, the people of Israel sinned against God . . . again. (Seriously, people? I'm gone for like a minute . . . .) When Nehemiah returned, he had to challenge them . . . again . . . to repent and follow God.

HOW NEHEMIAH EXCELLED AT WHAT HE DID

Nehemiah had a prominent position as cupbearer to King Artaxerxes. While that may sound like an insignificant role for a servant, it was actually a critical position in a king's administration. A cupbearer had to guard against a plot to kill the king by making sure none of the food or drinks were poisoned. As a result, the king had to have great trust and confidence in the cupbearer. Artaxerxes was king of the Persian Empire, which was one of the most powerful empires in history. Nehemiah must have been incredibly effective and trustworthy for such a powerful ruler to choose him for that role.

Nehemiah was clearly an effective planner. He didn't just show up and try to rebuild the walls of Jerusalem without a strategy. He put a plan in place to make it happen. He obtained critical resources from the king: letters for safe passage, a military escort, and wood to rebuild the city. Then, when he came to Jerusalem, he secretly inspected the walls of the city at night so he could create a plan before anyone knew he intended to rebuild the walls.[lxxiv]

Nehemiah was organized. He assigned specific groups to rebuild different parts of the walls and gates. He also organized a specific plan for security when they were threatened. He stationed guards behind the lowest parts of the wall and split the workers so that some worked while others held weapons. He had the men of Judah sleep inside the walls with their weapons by their sides in case they were attacked at night.[lxxv]

Nehemiah also excelled at challenging men. When some of the Jewish nobles were oppressing the poor, he challenged them to stop charging interest and return their land. When the nobles promised to return their land and stop oppressing them, Nehemiah didn't simply accept their promises. He called the priests and made the nobles swear they would keep their promises, which they did.[lxxvi] Later, Nehemiah had Ezra read the law to the people and celebrate the Feast of Booths as the law commanded. He also had the people confess their sins and the leaders make a written covenant to keep the law.[lxxvii] He even challenged the people who married foreign wives in disobedience of the Mosaic Law.[lxxviii] (Who knew foreign women were irresistible back then too? At least men are consistent.)

> In those days also I saw the Jews who had married women of Ashdod, Ammon, and Moab. And half of their children spoke the language of Ashdod, and they could not speak the language of Judah, but only the language of each people. And I confronted them and cursed them and beat some of them and pulled out their hair. And I made them take an oath in the name of God, saying, "You shall not give your daughters to their sons, or take their daughters for your sons or for yourselves." (Nehemiah 13:23-25)

I imagine that getting your hair pulled out by Nehemiah was not fun. This would be extreme by today's standards, but Nehemiah was so concerned that the people keep the law that he was willing to physically challenge men to keep God's commands.

Nehemiah was also a shrewd leader. The surrounding people tried repeatedly to set up a meeting with him so that they could kill him, but

Nehemiah did not fall for their tricks. He sent messengers back and simply refused to meet.[lxxix]

Nehemiah succeeded repeatedly where other men had failed. His life is a testament to what you can accomplish when you trust God.

Chapter 15

KEY POINTS ON EXCELLING AT WHAT YOU DO

TOUGH GUYS DIDN'T RUN AWAY FROM CONTROVERSY

The Tough Guys didn't excel because they avoided controversy; they excelled by taking it head on. When Pharaoh tasked Joseph with preparing for the famine, he taxed the people during the years of plenty. Nobody likes taxes. Even people who say they want higher taxes still hire accountants to pay the least amount possible. Levying taxes would not have been popular. But Joseph implemented this and saved the lives of many people as a result.

Nehemiah challenged the leaders of his day to stop marrying foreign wives.[39] Standing in the way of "love" is never popular. Imagine the heat he took for that one? He essentially called people's marriages unholy. That's a hard thing to accept about your marriage and even harder to hear about your children. Despite that, Nehemiah didn't shrink from the controversy. He came right out and challenged the men of Judah to follow God's commands about marriage.

---

39. God's command not to marry foreign wives was not a prohibition against inter-racial marriage. God didn't want the influence of people who worshiped false gods to cause the Israelites to go astray, which is exactly what happened to Solomon. See Deuteronomy 6 and 1 Kings 11. Both Rahab and Ruth were foreign women who feared God and were in the lineage of Jesus. They would only be in the line of Jesus if God allowed it, so we know God does not oppose inter-racial marriage.

Many of the Apostle Paul's letters include challenges to churches to stop their sinning. In ten of his thirteen letters, he challenged his readers on sexual sin. This is not an easy topic to discuss today, and I doubt it was any easier in Paul's day. However, he addressed it often because it was critical to making true disciples. He called out the Corinthian Church for its division, including lawsuits between believers.[lxxx] He even asked the Galatians if he had wasted his time on them.[lxxxi] Paul was an effective evangelist and missionary *because* he addressed controversial topics.

William Carey was a missionary to India in the early 1800s. Along with others, Carey fought aggressively to end the practice of Sati (burning a wife alive on her husband's funeral pyre). It's obvious now that was a horrific practice, but at the time, he was opposed by many Hindus who felt it was part of their religion. Carey worked for many years to make the practice illegal and even studied sacred Hindu texts to prove that Sati was not sanctioned by their religion. Carey could have just focused on telling people about Jesus, but he went beyond that and took on this controversial practice.[lxxxii]

EFFECTIVENESS LEADS TO INFLUENCE AND AUTHORITY

Joseph was given authority over Potiphar's house because he excelled at managing his estate.[lxxxiii] Joseph was given authority in the prison because he excelled at managing the prison.[lxxxiv] He was an effective manager, and people noticed. As a slave and later as a prisoner, he would normally have no influence or authority. However, his management skills made him a rock star. Joseph earned influence in the most unlikely places because he excelled in the tasks given to him.

Nehemiah was cupbearer to the Persian king even though he was a foreigner. He would not have been given that assignment unless he was incredibly effective and trustworthy. We clearly see Nehemiah's effectiveness in how he organized the people of Judah to rebuild the wall so quickly and also persuaded all the leaders to repent and return to God. Nehemiah showed up from Susa, and the people of Judah followed him. They could have rejected him as a carpet-bagging leader who was disloyal to the Jews since he served the Persian king who still held Judah as a conquered nation, but his competence clearly won them over.

One clear thing Nehemiah did was show up with a plan. When he asked the king for permission to take leave to go to Judah, he requested all the supplies and authority from the king that he would need. Then, when he arrived, he surveyed the city at night and created a plan before he presented it to anyone.[lxxxv] Men are more likely to follow you when you show up with a good plan. That takes time and attention to detail. Nehemiah did this well, which gave him influence and authority with the people of Judah.

Daniel's effectiveness also led to influence and authority. Even though he was a foreign slave, he gained influence within Babylon and later the Persian Empire. Nebuchadnezzar trusted him so much he put him in charge of Babylon.[lxxxvi] Later, when the Persians conquered Babylon, the ruler Darius made Daniel one of three high officials to rule over the entire kingdom and planned to elevate him over all the high officials.[lxxxvii] Not only was Daniel a foreign slave, he was also a leader within the now conquered Babylon. Normally such a person would be viewed with suspicion. Democrats don't typically keep the cabinet secretaries from the last Republican administration and vice versa. However, Daniel was so effective that leaders with many reasons not to trust him, still put him in positions of significant authority.

TOUGH GUYS DIDN'T ALWAYS HAVE WORLDLY SUCCESS

I often hear Christians say, "We've lost the culture" on certain issues, so we should just give up. They think there is no longer a point to encouraging our culture to live according to God's commands. These Christians misunderstand God's expectations of us. God doesn't call us to be successful. He calls us to be faithful. God can control our worldly success and failure. He'll use us how He sees fit according to His plans, which are better than our plans. God controls the worldly outcomes, not you. Your job is just to be faithful in following God's commands, which includes blessing the culture by promoting God's righteousness and not conforming to the world's "righteousness."

How often did the Israelites want to give up and go back to Egypt? (Spoiler alert if you haven't read the Old Testament—it happened a lot.) They lacked faith that God could deliver them from whatever crisis confronted them, so they looked to worldly saviors. I believe part of the reason God gave us all this detailed history in the Bible is so we won't fall into the same trap. We need to be faithful, trust God, and continue to follow His commands even when the situation looks hopeless.

The Tough Guys had many failures, but God didn't judge them on their success, or lack thereof, just on their faithfulness. Jeremiah gave Judah accurate warnings from God for forty years, and almost no one listened to him. After Nehemiah returned to Susa, the people of Judah started sinning again. John the Baptist was beheaded. Jesus was crucified and lost most of His followers. In the view of the world, He lost, but He actually won.

This is true for other Christians too. Bonhoeffer and MLK were both murdered in their thirties. The world thought they lost, but we still read their writings today. They both won.

Jonah (who was not a Tough Guy) had worldly success convincing the Ninevites to repent despite his unfaithfulness. He ran the other way when God commanded him to go to Nineveh and call them to repentance. There isn't a correlation between worldly success and faithfulness. Having a large church doesn't mean you're following God. Making a lot of money doesn't mean you're following God. Having an important leadership position doesn't mean you're following God. Throughout the Bible, God clearly blesses some Tough Guys with worldly success but gives other Tough Guys worldly struggles and failures. Don't worry about outcomes. You can't control them. You can only control whether you're faithful. To be faithful, you may have to sacrifice, and many people may not like you. But God loves you, and your faithfulness will please Him. His vote counts more than all the others combined.

TOUGH GUYS WERE SHREWD

The Tough Guys didn't just work hard. They were also shrewd. They made good choices that helped them succeed. Nehemiah wasn't fooled by the men in Judah who tried to trick him into meeting so they could kill him. He refused to meet and stayed focused on the work of rebuilding the wall.

Joseph used the stored grain to buy up all the land from people and made Pharaoh even richer in the process. Daniel asked Nebuchadnezzar to have his countrymen Shadrach, Meshach, and Abednego work for him. He put people he could trust into positions of leadership. All Christian men should learn from these examples. We should be shrewd as well. Jesus even told a parable about a shrewd manager to make this point.

He also said to the disciples, "There was a rich man who had a manager, and charges were brought to him that this man was wasting his possessions. And he called him and said to him, 'What is this that I hear about you? Turn in the account of your management, for you can no longer be manager.' And the manager said to himself, 'What shall I do, since my master is taking the management away from me? I am not strong enough to dig, and I am ashamed to beg. I have decided what to do, so that when I am removed from management, people may receive me into their houses.' So, summoning his master's debtors one by one, he said to the first, 'How much do you owe my master?' He said, 'A hundred measures of oil.' He said to him, 'Take your bill, and sit down quickly and write fifty.' Then he said to another, 'And how much do you owe?' He said, 'A hundred measures of wheat.' He said to him, 'Take your bill, and write eighty.' The master commended the dishonest manager for his shrewdness. For the sons of this world are more shrewd in dealing with their own generation than the sons of light." (Luke 16:1-8)

In the parable, even though the manager is dishonest, the rich man calls him shrewd. Jesus went on to say, "The sons of this world are more shrewd . . . than the sons of light." I don't think Jesus was excusing or condoning the manager's dishonesty. However, I do think Jesus challenged us to be shrewd in dealing with other people.

We should love our neighbors as ourselves, but that doesn't mean we have to allow others to take advantage of us. We don't expect our neighbors to allow others to take advantage of them. In fact, if we see someone exploiting our neighbor, we should speak up and intervene. Likewise, if someone tries to exploit us, we should speak up. We don't have to take it like a doormat. You don't have to lose all the time to be a Christian (even though pop culture would have you think that). The Tough Guys showed us we can be clever and shrewd in dealing with people while still following God's commands. I'm not suggesting you should use shrewdness and go right up to the edge of violating God's commands. This is not a balancing act. I'm suggesting you should use shrewdness, as the Tough Guys did, specifically to accomplish God's will.

IDLENESS IS SINFUL

God designed us to work. God commanded us to work, starting in Genesis, even before Adam sinned.[lxxxviii] This command was repeated in the New Testament. The Apostle Paul commanded us to have nothing to do with those who are idle.

Now we command you, brothers, in the name of our Lord Jesus Christ, that you keep away from any brother who is walking in idleness and not in accord with the tradition that you received from us. (2 Thessalonians 3:6)

If the Apostle Paul were writing that today, he might say, "Keep away from any brother who spends all his time playing video games." If you're not using the gifts God gave you to work and serve His kingdom as well as others, you're sinning. You can't just opt out of everything and take care of yourself.

In one neighborhood where I lived in New York City, I would often see a disabled man walking to work. He walked with a crutch because his right foot was sideways, and his right leg was shorter than his left. He struggled to take every step. Just walking somewhere was a lot of work for him, but he did it. Every time I saw him, it reminded me how easy God made my life. I can accomplish most of the things I need to live with ease. Watching this disabled man work so hard just to get to work inspired me not to be idle with my time. He wasn't idle. He was constantly working hard to accomplish even small things. Just because I could finish my work faster than he, didn't mean I could go and be idle the rest of the time. The ease of my life was a blessing from God. I should use the extra time that blessing created to be productive for Him and not just binge on Netflix or play video games.

I doubt Joseph and Nehemiah had much downtime in their days. Based on what they accomplished, they were likely working sunup to sundown. You couldn't accomplish all those things and go through life at a leisurely pace. If you want to be like the Tough Guys, don't be idle. You should take time for rest, as the Bible commands us, but don't waste time on trivial pursuits. Use your time to serve God and bless others.

DON'T BE A FIVE-TALENT MAN WITH ONE-TALENT RESULTS

God gives each of us talents to use for His kingdom. In Matthew 25, Jesus told the parable of the talents. You've likely read it (and should, if you haven't), but here is a quick recap: A master went on a journey but first left three of his servants with five, two, and one talents,[40] respectively. The first servant turned the five talents into five more. Likewise, the second servant turned the two talents into two more. However, the third servant took his talent and hid it away and gave it back to his master upon his return. The master praised the first two servants, but read how he addressed the last servant:

> *"He also who had received the one talent came forward, saying, 'Master, I knew you to be a hard man, reaping where you did not sow, and gathering where you scattered no seed, so I was afraid, and*

---

40. In New Testament times, a *talent* was a financial unit of measurement equal to roughly twenty years of wages for a laborer. In this parable, Jesus uses a financial measurement to illustrate how men should use the actual talents and capabilities God has given them.

I went and hid your talent in the ground. Here, you have what is yours.' But his master answered him, 'You wicked and slothful servant! *You knew that I reap where I have not sown and gather where I scattered no seed? Then you ought to have invested my money with the bankers, and at my coming I should have received what was my own with interest. So take the talent from him and give it to him who has the ten talents. For to everyone who has will more be given, and he will have an abundance. But from the one who has not, even what he has will be taken away.* And cast the worthless servant into the outer darkness. *In that place there will be weeping and gnashing of teeth.'" (Matthew 25:24-30)*

The master called the servant *wicked and slothful* for not using the talent given to him. God gives us our talents for a purpose. He wants us to use them for His kingdom. Many of you reading this may be like the servant given five talents. Don't use that to serve yourself or give yourself an easy life; use those talents to serve God. Even if you think you're like the one-talent servant (and you're probably underestimating yourself), you still need to use that talent to serve God.

Nehemiah was clearly a five-talent man. He could have just lived a cushy life as cupbearer in the king's administration. He didn't have to use his talents to serve God, but he did. If he just kept his cushy life as a cupbearer, he likely wouldn't be in the Bible. He's in the Bible because he did invest his talents in God's kingdom. Likewise, Joseph was a five-talent guy. When Potiphar put him in prison, he could have done the minimum. Who would blame him for getting bitter after all the injustice done to him? However, he responded by continuing to use his talents to serve in the situation in which God put him. It eventually led to God giving him an enormous assignment as Prime Minister of Egypt. Perhaps God needed to know he would be faithful in a small role before He gave him a big one?

God gave you talents. Be like the Tough Guys and use them to serve Him and others. Bless your community, your church, your country, and your family by using your talents even when your Master is away.

TOUGH GUYS CAN BE ANY AGE

You're never too young to be a Tough Guy, and it's never too late to start. Throughout the Bible, God called Tough Guys to serve Him at many different ages. Jeremiah was a youth when he was called.[lxxxix] King David was a teenager when he killed Goliath.[xc] JTB was in his twenties when he started his ministry. Joseph was just seventeen when he was sold into slavery and only thirty when he was made the Prime Minister of Egypt. On the other hand, Daniel was likely in his eighties when he was put in the lions' den. Likewise, Moses was around eighty when God called him to go confront Pharaoh.

God can use you at any age to help fulfill His plans. If you think you're too young to make an impact, you're not. You can take risks, speak the truth directly, excel at what you do, and fear God more than men. If you're willing to do that, God can use you. God may not put you on a stage as big as the *Tough Guys of the Bible*, but that doesn't mean you won't have an impact. Don't judge your ministry using worldly standards. Let God use you, and you'll accomplish exactly what He has set out for you.

If you think you're too old to start being a Tough Guy, you're not. I'm sure Moses thought he would just be a shepherd for the rest of his life. I doubt he could have imagined the many wondrous miracles God would work through him for the last forty years of his life.

> *Moses was 120 years old when he died. His eye was undimmed, and his vigor unabated. (Deuteronomy 34:7)*

It's not natural to have strength until you're 120. God clearly gave Moses that strength. (Imagine getting beat up by a 120-year-old guy. Your friends would never let you live it down.) He can do the same thing for you. If God wants to use you to accomplish something, and you truly trust Him, He will give you everything you need to make it happen.

Don't use your age as an excuse. Start living like the Tough Guys now. Let God use you for His purposes. You won't regret it.

WHAT IS YOUR GOAL AS A CHRISTIAN?

Most men have goals for different aspects of their life. They want to win a championship or set a record in sports. They want to make a certain amount of money. They want to open a great restaurant. They want to get elected mayor of their town.

There is nothing wrong with these goals. God can use you in all those places to do amazing things. However, those are worldly goals. What goals have you set as a Christian? How many other men do you want to disciple? How much money do you want to give to your church? How many fatherless children do you want to mentor?

Most successful men don't stumble into their success. They set goals and pursue them deliberately. They use milestones to measure their progress. They read books to gain subject matter expertise. They seek advice from older men on how to be more effective. Why wouldn't you use the same approach in serving God? You should set goals and keep track of the results. Of course you should start with prayer and ask God what He wants you to do. Some men get very direct answers, and other men have to go through a process of trial and error. If you don't get a direct answer, that's OK. Use your wisdom and try something. If God opens the door and blesses it, keep going. If not, try something else. If your career wasn't going well, you wouldn't just keep doing the same thing. You would re-evaluate and take a different approach. Do the same thing with your Christian goals.

You can see this trial-and-error approach in the life of Paul.

> *And they went through the region of Phrygia and Galatia, having been forbidden by the Holy Spirit to speak the word in Asia. And when they had come up to Mysia, they attempted to go into Bithynia, but the Spirit of Jesus did not allow them. So, passing by Mysia, they went down to Troas. And a vision appeared to Paul in the night: a man of Macedonia was standing there, urging him and saying, "Come over to Macedonia and help us." And when Paul had seen the vision, immediately we sought to go on into Macedonia, concluding that God had called us to preach the gospel to them. (Act 16:6-10)*

Paul would try to go somewhere, but if the Holy Spirit prevented him, he would go somewhere else. He didn't give up; he kept trying other approaches to find success. The other thing this passage proves is that Paul didn't always know where God wanted him to go. Sometimes he would just go and see if God blessed it or prevented it. If Paul, who had an incredible prophetic gift, didn't always know where God wanted him to go, then you shouldn't expect to always know either. If your plan is failing, move on and try something else.

One final point on this topic. All those worldly accomplishments, for which you make plans, will only pay off in this life—which isn't long. Your accomplishments for the kingdom of God will pay off forever. If you could divide ninety-five (a long life) by infinity (eternity in heaven), it would be a really small percentage of your entire life. Make sure you're setting goals as a Christian to accomplish things for God. If you're not having success, try something else until it's clear you're doing what God wants you to do.

Chapter 16

PASTOR'S LOG: OVERCOMING CHALLENGES AND PREJUDICE THROUGH EXCELLENCE

RYAN: INCREDIBLY PRODUCTIVE DESPITE HIS PHYSICAL LIMITATIONS

Ryan[41] was a junior high school teacher (probably the most unappreciated job in the world other than maybe roadkill collector or pet food taster), and his wife was a school nurse. One day, while swimming in a lake, Ryan dove in and hit his head. He broke his neck and almost drowned. He survived only because his wife jumped in and saved him. As a result of the accident, he was almost a quadriplegic, with no use of his legs and very limited use of his hands. During recovery, he had to spend several months in a stretcher that rotated him so he didn't develop bed sores. After he was out of the hospital, his wife set her alarm for 2 a.m. every night to rotate him. God clearly gifted Ryan with an amazing wife.

Many men who suffered that kind of injury might become bitter at life and at God, but not Ryan. As soon as he recovered, he returned to teaching junior high school. He was an excellent teacher. His students would arrive early to come help him out of the car and wheel him into the classroom. If you don't remember junior high, that's when nice kids turn

---

41. Pseudonym used to protect the individual's identity.

into obnoxious teenagers and generally treat their teachers with disdain. To have junior high kids volunteer to help a disabled teacher is a testament to how much his students loved him.

Beyond teaching, Ryan had a keen ear for music. He was captivated with pipe organs, so he contacted a local high school and hired two boys. From his wheelchair, he taught the boys how to assemble a pipe organ in his home. Then, the guy who could barely move his arms became active in a guild of organ players, some of whom would come from all around the world to give recitals. Many other people would come listen, and Ryan used this as an opportunity to tell people about Jesus. He was a phenomenal evangelist from his wheelchair.

Later, he wanted to create a Christmas light display at his house. He hired some kids to put up one hundred thousand lights at his house. Thousands of people would show up to see it, and he used that as an opportunity to tell them about Jesus.

Ryan's town eventually told him he could no longer put up his light display at home, so his church allowed him to light up their building. He expanded the Christmas display to five hundred thousand lights initially and over one million in later years. Even more people would come, which gave Ryan even more opportunities to tell people about Jesus.

Ryan lost the use of most of his body but still had a great outlook on life. He was never angry. Most people knew him to be a lighthearted jokester. Rather than focus on the abilities he lost, Ryan leveraged the remaining abilities God had given him to do even more. He excelled at teaching and organizing and used those abilities to bless people with music and light shows that tens of thousands enjoyed. He leveraged his engaging personality to witness to many people. He accomplished more from a wheelchair than most men have accomplished with full use of their arms and legs. Ryan was a real-life Tough Guy who excelled at what he did to serve God, despite incredible challenges.

JOHN WOODEN: LEVERAGING SUCCESS TO PROMOTE JUSTICE

One of the most successful college basketball coaches of all time, John Wooden, led his teams to ten NCAA championships and won more than 80 percent of his games as a head coach from 1946 to 1975. He's also one of only four people inducted into the Basketball Hall of Fame as both a player and a coach. His approach to coaching is legendary and has been taught in many different books over the years.

Wooden was a Christian man with incredible character he learned from his father. This character came into play during his first two years as a head coach at Indiana State University.[42] In the first season (1946–47), he led the team to a 17-8 record, which earned the team an invitation to the NAIB[43] tournament; but the invitation came with a stipulation. The team could not bring one player, Clarence Walker, because he was Black. At the time, the NAIB, and other college sports associations, didn't allow Black players to participate in their tournaments. Wooden declined the invitation.

You might be thinking that Wooden didn't want to enter the arena without his best player, but Walker was not even a starter. It would have been easy for Wooden to justify leaving him behind. It's unlikely it would have significantly impacted his team's performance. It was also likely very disappointing to the other players who had worked so hard to have a winning season. In addition, this was Wooden's first head coaching job. Most men would not want to "make waves" that early in their career, but Wooden was resolute that either all or none of his players would participate. He wasn't willing to exclude Clarence because of his race.

The next season, Wooden coached the team to an even better 27-7 record. Again, the team received an invitation to the NAIB tournament. They agreed to allow Walker to play but said he couldn't stay in the same hotel or eat with the team. Wooden again declined the invitation. He still wasn't willing to exclude one of his players from any aspect of the tournament. However, the NAACP[44] contacted Wooden and asked him to reconsider. Clarence would be the first Black player to participate in the NAIB tournament, and they saw this as an opportunity for a civil rights breakthrough. This was only one year after Jackie Robinson joined the Brooklyn Dodgers and sixteen years before Congress passed the Civil Rights Act of 1964. The NAACP had lined up a local pastor who would host Clarence with his family. Under these circumstances, Wooden agreed that the team could play.

As a result of this breakthrough, the next year (1949), three teams brought Black players to the NAIB tournament. In 1950, City College of New York won both the NIT and NCAA tournaments with two Black starters after both tournaments followed the NAIB's lead in ending the ban on Black players. Wooden's decision to treat Walker with dignity and choose justice over the potential glory of a successful tournament contributed to

42. It was Indiana State Teachers College when Wooden coached there but later became Indiana State University.

43. National Association for Intercollegiate Basketball. This was before most college sports leagues were consolidated under the NCAA.

44. National Association for the Advancement of Colored People (NAACP)

the integration of college basketball. He did not know it at the time, but he would go on to win more NCAA basketball tournaments than any other coach in history.

What's critical about this story is that Wooden had this opportunity to promote justice because of his success. Had he coached the team to a 7-27 record instead of a 27-7 record, no one would have cared about his demand to allow Clarence to play. In fact, it's very unlikely the team would have even received an invitation to the tournament. Wooden's success as a basketball coach gave him the opportunity to promote a positive change in our society. Wooden excelled in his role as a coach, and that gave him the influence to promote justice. But he also wasn't afraid to forgo opportunities for success to live like Jesus. That makes him a Tough Guy. Be like Coach Wooden: use the talents and skills God gave you to excel so that you'll also have opportunities to influence our society to conform to the commands of the Bible.[xci]

Chapter 17

JESUS EXCELLED
TO SERVE OTHERS

T his one feels like an unfair comparison since Jesus was God. He was
the author of Creation. How could He not excel in the world He
created? He literally wrote the playbook. However, do not forget that Jesus
was both fully God and fully man. He shared our human weaknesses and
yet still excelled at what He did.

Jesus also made clear we can do even greater works than He if we have
faith.

> *"Truly, truly, I say to you, whoever believes in me will also do the
> works that I do; and greater works than these will he do, because I
> am going to the Father." (John 14:12)*

Of course, we will never live perfect lives like Jesus, but that doesn't
mean we can't strive to excel at all the things we do like He did. Since He
gave us the Holy Spirit to help us, we can accomplish great things that may
seem impossible on our own.

One area where Jesus excelled was healing. Jesus didn't just heal a few
people. In many cases, the Bible tells us He healed everyone who came.

That evening they brought to him many who were oppressed by demons, and he cast out the spirits with a word and healed all who were sick. (Matthew 8:16)

Jesus, aware of this, withdrew from there. And many followed him, and he healed them all and ordered them not to make him known. (Matthew 12:15-16)

Now when the sun was setting, all those who had any who were sick with various diseases brought them to him, and he laid his hands on every one of them and healed them. (Luke 4:40)

The point here is not that Jesus had (and continues to have) the supernatural ability to heal, it's that He took the time to heal everyone. This is a model for us. When you use your talents from God, do you share them that way? Are you diligent enough to do the whole job and not just half of it? Jesus did the whole job. You should too.

Jesus excelled at teaching. People flocked to hear what Jesus had to say. Even two thousand years later, His teaching is incredibly clear. He used parables and direct language to make it easier for all of us to understand.

Jesus was a phenomenal debater. The Pharisees and Sadducees challenged Him frequently and tried to catch Him in contradictions or violations of the Jewish law, but Jesus always had great responses.

Then the Pharisees went and plotted how to entangle him in his words. And they sent their disciples to him, along with the Herodians, saying, "Teacher, we know that you are true and teach the way of God truthfully, and you do not care about anyone's opinion, for you are not swayed by appearances. Tell us, then, what you think. Is it lawful to pay taxes to Caesar, or not?" But Jesus, aware of their malice, said, "Why put me to the test, you hypocrites? Show me the coin for the tax." And they brought him a denarius. And Jesus said to them, "Whose likeness and inscription is this?" They said, "Caesar's." Then he said to them, "Therefore render to Caesar the things that are Caesar's, and to God the things that are God's." When they heard it, they marveled. And they left him and went away. (Matthew 22:15-22)

This was a mic drop moment. I like to think that after they left, Jesus said to the crowd, "Bring it!" I know that's not in the Bible, but it doesn't mean Jesus wasn't thinking it. That will be one of my many questions in heaven.

You may think that Jesus used His supernatural gifts to outsmart these religious leaders, but there is evidence He prepared just as any other man would. Luke 2 recounts the story of Jesus staying behind in Jerusalem to spend time at the temple.

After three days they found him in the temple, sitting among the teachers, listening to them and asking them questions. And all who heard him were amazed at his understanding and his answers. (Luke 2:46-47)

Jesus started listening to religious teachers and asking questions at age twelve (and maybe earlier). He was listening *and* asking questions. He was preparing to teach and debate. If Jesus relied solely on His supernatural gifts, He wouldn't have had to do that. He clearly studied as a man. Jesus was intentional in His preparation. We can be intentional as well. Whatever mission God has given you, start preparing right away. Take the time to develop expertise so you can excel in whatever God has planned for you.

PART V

THEY FEARED GOD MORE THAN MEN

Chapter 18

ELIJAH: FIRE FROM HEAVEN

| 863 BC | **Elijah** Prayed for Drought |

BACKGROUND ON ELIJAH

E lijah lived about two hundred years after Gideon's battle with the Midianites and Amalekites and one hundred years after King David died. At this point, a civil war had already divided Israel into Ephraim and Judah. As a prophet, Elijah challenged the kings of Ephraim—first Ahab and then Ahaziah (Ahab's son). Ahab, along with his wife Jezebel, worshiped the pagan idol Baal and his mother, the fertility goddess Asherah, the same false gods the Israelites worshiped in Gideon's time (bad habits are hard to break). Ahab's wickedness went beyond idol worship.

> *And Ahab the son of Omri did evil in the sight of the Lord, more than all who were before him. And as if it had been a light thing for him to walk in the sins of Jeroboam the son of Nebat, he took for his wife Jezebel the daughter of Ethbaal king of the Sidonians, and went and served Baal and worshiped him. He erected an altar for Baal in the house of Baal, which he built in Samaria. And Ahab made an Asherah. Ahab did more to provoke the Lord, the God of Israel, to anger than all the kings of Israel who were before him. (1 Kings 16:30-33)*

All the kings of Ephraim were wicked, so Ahab had to work pretty hard to be more wicked than all those before him (excellent work, Ahab![45]). Ahab's son Ahaziah also worshiped Baal but reigned for less than two years because of God's judgment on him.

The Bible gives us no information about Elijah's upbringing other than that he was a Tishbite from a place called Gilead. During his life, Elijah served God faithfully. God used Elijah to perform many miracles. Elijah accurately prophesied that there would be no rain for three years. He raised a boy from the dead. He prayed and God set fire to a wet altar (which would have been really useful in Boy Scout camp after a thunderstorm). He ran faster than a chariot (too bad this was before the Olympics were invented). God also protected Elijah by sending fire to destroy soldiers sent to kill him, after which Elijah said, "Anyone else want a piece of me?" There is actually no record in the Bible of Elijah saying this, but, come on, he was a dude. Dudes did as dudes do even three thousand years ago.

Elijah never died. God took him directly into heaven. The Bible only records this privilege for one other man: Enoch. (In light of that, you would think that both of these names would be more popular.) Before he left, Elijah anointed Elisha as his successor. Throughout his life, Elijah always responded to God's call to serve. He took many risks and had faith that God would protect him. Most of what we know about Elijah can be found in 1 Kings 17 through 2 Kings 2.

HOW ELIJAH FEARED GOD MORE THAN MEN

For his first recorded act as a prophet, Elijah told King Ahab that because of his wickedness, it would not rain until Elijah said so[xcii] (which makes me wonder if Elijah has been hanging out in CA recently). A famine came, and Ahab had his army search every country for Elijah with orders to kill him; but God protected him.[xciii] In addition to the physical risk, this would have been emotionally stressful for Elijah. Imagine if the KGB, Russian Police, and Russian Military were all searching for you at the same time. You would have to be vigilant every moment of every day. You couldn't make a mistake or someone might recognize you and turn you in for a significant reward. This was Elijah's life for more than three years. While he knew God protected him, keep in mind we know that God is protecting us, and yet we stress out about much smaller problems.

---

45. To minimize the number of angry emails, I want to point out that this is sarcasm.

Have you ever worked for a company that announced layoffs were coming? Think about how much stress you felt as you wondered whether you might lose your job. Losing your job is rough, but most of the time, you will be able to handle the challenge. You will typically be out of work for a period of time and then find another job. It may dent your savings, and you might have to move to find a new job, but you will survive. Now imagine, instead, that if you get laid off, they kill you. That would raise the stakes. That would count as a significant problem. Now imagine living with that uncertainty every day for more than three years. That was Elijah's life. If caught, Ahab could have executed him. Elijah lived with that stress every day, and yet he still feared God more than he feared Ahab.

Do you have that kind of faithfulness when the stakes are much lower? Do you follow God's commands when the cost of obedience is so much smaller? I've often had conversations with men who claim Christianity who try to justify sinful behavior by saying, "I had no choice." Typically, they attempt to justify their dishonesty or exploitation with excuses such as, "I have to feed my family." They feared the worldly consequences of following God's commands more than they feared God. Sadly, these men often earn salaries at the upper end of the economic spectrum, live in nice homes, and drive expensive cars. The "cost" they fear isn't their family starving or eviction from their home. Usually they worry that they might not get a promotion or a large bonus. They had no choice because they fear losing the favor of the gods of money or power. They didn't fear the God of the Bible who told them to love their neighbors as themselves. Elijah risked so much more than money, career, or status, and yet he feared God more than the king. We should all strive to do the same.

What's amazing about Elijah's story is that he continued to fear God even as God repeatedly asked him to risk death. This wasn't a one-time request. Elijah constantly had to choose between fearing God and fearing Ahab. After more than three years of drought, God told Elijah to go confront Ahab. Ahab! The king who wanted to kill him. When God first commanded this, Elijah likely responded, "Ahab who? Ahab Johnson, Ahab Smith? There are a lot of Ahabs." The Bible does not record any such response by Elijah, but you can imagine that he had serious concerns with following out that command.

Imagine going to confront the Russian president who sent out the KGB and military to hunt you down and bury you where no one would find you. That is the last person you would want to see. It would take tremendous courage to follow that command. If your friend found himself in that situation and told you he planned to travel to Moscow, you would advise him not to go. You would call it a suicide mission, but Elijah went.

Not only did Elijah go and confront the king, but he challenged him to a battle between Ahab's god (Baal) and the true God of Israel. Elijah told him to call all the people of Israel. [xciv] Then he had the prophets of Baal build an altar to their god and pray for fire while he built an altar and prayed to the true God.[xcv] There were four hundred fifty prophets of Baal versus just Elijah.[xcvi]

Think about how much confidence it must have taken for Elijah to stand alone against all those prophets in addition to the soldiers and the people of Israel who worshiped this false god. How many times in your life have you been alone in an argument against four or five men and failed to hold your ground even when you knew you were right? Did you fold after it became obvious you weren't going to change anyone's mind? Do you think you would have the confidence to take on a crowd of thousands or maybe tens of thousands armed with nothing but the clothes on your back? What's even more amazing is that Elijah didn't stand there in fear, hoping that God would somehow get him out of this situation alive. He possessed so much confidence in God that he actually mocked the other prophets when Baal failed to send fire.

> *And at noon Elijah mocked them, saying, "Cry aloud, for he is a god. Either he is musing, or he is relieving himself, or he is on a journey, or perhaps he is asleep and must be awakened." (1 Kings 18:27)*

Elijah told the prophets and the soldiers and all the people of Ephraim that their god isn't responding because he might be going to the bathroom or may be asleep or maybe he took a vacation. That is bold!

In New York City, some sports bars always show a particular college football team on Saturday. Many of the fans of that team (let's say USC, for example) will congregate in that sports bar to watch the game. On those days, almost everyone in the bar is a fan of USC. If USC didn't even show up for the game, what do you think would happen if a fan of UCLA came in and started mocking them? I don't mean taunting them by saying, "UCLA rules!" or "USC stinks!" I mean mocking them by saying, "Maybe everyone on your team is constipated and stuck in the bathroom," or, "Maybe your team just forgot to wake up this morning." What do you think would happen if a UCLA fan used that kind of language? It would not be very long before that guy was thoroughly beaten up and thrown out of the bar in a way designed to inflict the most amount of pain.

But Elijah didn't mock their sports team. He mocked their god—the entity they worshiped. The thing they believed provided them with protection, food, and prosperity. He didn't just accuse their god of not responding. He went beyond that and said offensive things about their god. This was a very personal insult, yet Elijah said it anyway. He knew he had God and truth on his side. Imagine if every Christian man had that kind of confidence in God. If we had faith that He would protect us against huge crowds even when we stood alone, how much bolder would we be? How much more effective would we be in everything that we do? Christian men could accomplish great things with that kind of faith.

Of course, the altar to Baal didn't catch fire. Then Elijah had the prophets drench his altar with water (just to mock their god a little more)[xcvii] before he prayed. God sent fire to Elijah's altar, and the people of Israel responded. They didn't just start to respect God. They didn't just decide to add God to the list of gods they worshiped. They did a complete reversal and turned on Baal. Elijah commanded them to seize the false prophets and kill them. Moved by the display of God's power, the Israelites obeyed.[xcviii] They started to fear God more than all these false prophets. This one supernatural act by God gave Elijah tremendous authority with the people. Imagine if we really gave our lives to God, how He could use us.

Elijah continued to fear God even after the death of Ahab. After Ahaziah became king, God commanded Elijah to challenge him. Ahaziah had injured himself in a fall, and rather than inquire of God whether he would recover, he sent messengers to inquire of a false god. This was after Elijah had shown through the demonstration of the two altars that the God of the Bible was the true God. Ahaziah was Ahab's son and would likely have known this story (and may have even been there). Yet he still decided to seek the counsel of false gods. (*Seriously?*)[xcix] Elijah met the men and delivered a message from the true God that Ahaziah would not recover.[c] Enraged, Ahaziah sent fifty soldiers to capture Elijah.[ci] Incredibly, Elijah just sat on top of a hill. Even though he could see the soldiers coming, he didn't run away or try to hide. He just waited with confidence. In fact, the soldiers came close enough to have a conversation with Elijah. If fifty armed men came out to get you, would you have the courage to sit and wait until they were so close that you could talk to them? Wouldn't you try to run away while you had a head start? Most men would flee, but Elijah feared God more than fifty soldiers, so he stayed.

The captain demanded that Elijah come down, but instead Elijah called for fire from heaven and it consumed the soldiers.[cii] (The fire from heaven thing really comes in handy sometimes.) Undeterred, Ahaziah sent another fifty soldiers.[ciii] You have to hand it to Ahaziah. Fire from heaven would convince most kings to discontinue their mission. But not Ahaziah. He kept going. Elijah again called for fire from heaven which consumed the soldiers.[civ] Blinded by power (or stupidity), Ahaziah sent a third group of fifty soldiers. (They must have been thrilled with that order.)[cv] The third captain valued his life, so he bowed down and begged Elijah not to send fire to consume them. (I'm not sure they taught the groveling maneuver at ancient military academies, but it worked out for this guy.)[cvi] The angel of the Lord told Elijah to go with them, and he confronted Ahaziah, telling him correctly he would die for worshiping a false god.[cvii] Elijah went and confronted the very man who had just sent a total of one hundred fifty soldiers to kill him. It's hard to imagine what kind of courage that would have taken. However, Elijah feared the consequences of not following God's commands more than he feared Ahaziah. He knew the king could not hurt him unless God allowed it.

Whenever men are pressuring you to go against God's commands and you're fearful of the consequences, just think of Elijah. He had a healthy fear of God that all men should have.

Chapter 19

STEPHEN: FEARING GOD, LOVING THE LOST

| 31 AD | Stoning of **Stephen** |

BACKGROUND ON STEPHEN

S tephen's life overlapped with the life and ministry of Jesus, although it is unclear whether they ever met. He's not mentioned in the Bible until shortly after Jesus ascends into heaven. Stephen's name means "victor's crown," and he wore it well as he boldly preached the truth of the gospel. He was first mentioned in Acts 6 when the Hellenists complained about the lack of support for their widows. The Hellenists were Jews who were likely born in other countries (or descended from Jews born in other countries) and would have spoken Greek rather than Aramaic. Having grown up in other parts of the world, the Hellenists adopted parts of the Greek culture so there was tension between the Hebrews (native to Judea) and the Hellenists. To address the concern about the lack of support for the Hellenist widows, seven men, including Stephen, were selected to attend to this and effectively play the role of deacons.[46] All seven had Greek names, which suggests they were Hellenists rather than Hebrews.

---

46. The term *deacon* doesn't show up in the Bible until Paul writes his letter to the Philippians (Philippians 1:1) and his first letter to Timothy (1 Timothy 3:8-13) approximately thirty years later, but these seven men are now thought of as the first Christian deacons.

Stephen likely only played this role for a short time and then moved on to using his supernatural gifts as part of an evangelistic ministry. Just a few verses after he was installed as a deacon, Stephen started debating the Scriptures with men from the synagogue of the Freedman.[47] Unable to compete with Stephen's wisdom, these men spread lies about him and had him brought before the Sanhedrin Council,[48] charging him with speaking against the temple and the Law of Moses. Stephen proceeded to make his defense by giving the Council a history lesson of the disobedience of the Jewish people and accusing the Council of murdering the Messiah just as their ancestors had murdered the prophets who had prophesied the coming of Jesus. Enraged, the Council took him out of the city and stoned him. In his last recorded words, Stephen asked God not to hold his murder against his fellow Jews.

HOW STEPHEN FEARED GOD MORE THAN MEN

Most of what we know about Stephen comes from Acts 6–7. There aren't a lot of words devoted to Stephen, but even the few we do have speak volumes about his character and strength. The men selected to lead the benevolence ministry had to be of good repute,[49] full of the Holy Spirit and full of wisdom. Stephen must have had these characteristics since he made the cut. We also know he was full of wisdom and the Holy Spirit because of his interactions with other men.

> *Then some of those who belonged to the synagogue of the Freedmen (as it was called), and of the Cyrenians, and of the Alexandrians, and of those from Cilicia and Asia, rose up and disputed with Stephen. But they could not withstand the wisdom and the Spirit with which he was speaking. (Acts 6:9-10)*

No one could challenge Stephen's wisdom in a debate because the Holy Spirit was with him. Stephen debated and challenged a lot of different people—men from the synagogue of the Freedman, the Cyrenians, the Alexandrians, as well as men from Cilicia and Asia. Stephen didn't back down from proclaiming Christ to these men who clearly didn't believe him and didn't want to hear it. (Very few people who are wrong do want to "hear it.")

The Bible says these men stirred people up against Stephen and later had false witnesses testify against him. It is clear Stephen didn't back down

---

47. Jews who had been Roman slaves and were later freed.
48. Jewish religious leaders
49. My wife hates the choice of this word, but it's in the Bible and I'm appealing to a Higher Authority in this case. It means they had to have a good reputation.

at all from challenging these men. When you're in a debate with a group of people, you can typically tell when they're starting to get upset. You know when things are getting heated. At that point, you have to make a choice about whether to keep pushing or to de-escalate the situation. A lot of times, men will say something like, "We'll just have to agree to disagree," but Stephen didn't do that. He kept pushing. He was more concerned with pleasing God by proclaiming the truth of Jesus than he was with pacifying these men. Stephen likely understood these men presented a physical threat to him, but that didn't stop him from challenging them.

Later, when he was brought before the Sanhedrin Council, Stephen did the most incredible thing. First, he gave these religious leaders and scholars a history lesson. They must have been incredulous. This is like a college freshman going into the history department faculty lounge and saying, "Let me explain the Middle Ages to you." I'm sure some of the people listening were thinking, *No he didn't! No he didn't just say that!* To say this was bold would be an understatement.

However, Stephen didn't stop there. He went on to accuse these religious leaders of murder and failing to keep the law—and keeping the law was totally their thing. The men must have been shocked. They must have thought, *Who does this guy think he is?*

Jesus warned His disciples about situations like this.

"And when they bring you before the synagogues and the rulers and the authorities, do not be anxious about how you should defend yourself or what you should say, for the Holy Spirit will teach you in that very hour what you ought to say." (Luke 12:11-12)

It's not clear if Stephen would have heard Jesus say this, but he clearly followed the command. Stephen was full of the Holy Spirit and gave one of the longest and most effective sermons in the Bible in front of an audience of rulers who wanted to kill him . . . and eventually did. Stephen feared God more than this group of powerful men.

When these men took him out of the city and stoned him to death, Stephen's reaction was even more courageous: he asked God to forgive them. How tough do you have to be to feel no vengeance against the people murdering you and ask God not to hold that sin against them? Stephen was full of love for these men at the same time he was full of the fear of the Lord. He didn't fear these men but instead loved them and sought their salvation. Even though Stephen was a martyr and is often portrayed as a victim, Stephen was a tough man. It took tremendous courage to do what he did.

Unlike Elijah, Stephen is not delivered from his earthly enemies. One of the lessons from the lives of Elijah and Stephen is that we need to fear God more than men and let God decide the outcomes. Whether He delivers us from earthly dangers or allows us to be harmed or even murdered, we still need to fear Him, just like the Tough Guys.

Chapter 20

KEY POINTS ON FEARING GOD MORE THAN MEN

JUDGMENT IS REAL

I think the reason many Christian men don't fear God more than men is they don't truly believe God's judgment is real. They haven't come to terms with the idea that there are consequences for disobeying God. We know God is love, but that didn't stop Jesus from talking about judgment.[cviii]

When Jesus sent His disciples out to the cities of Israel, He told them what would happen to towns that rejected His message.

> *And if anyone will not receive you or listen to your words, shake off the dust from your feet when you leave that house or town. Truly, I say to you, it will be more bearable on the day of judgment for the land of Sodom and Gomorrah than for that town. (Matthew 10:14-15)*

You might think to yourself, *What could be worse than having your city destroyed by fire from heaven?* Read Revelation. It can get worse . . . much, much worse. This passage is one of the many times Jesus talked about judgment. One day we will all have to answer to *that* Jesus.

> *For we must all appear before the judgment seat of Christ, so that each one may receive what is due for what he has done in the body, whether good or evil. (2 Corinthians 5:10)*

I took a skydiving class once. One of the other students asked what would happen if his parachute didn't open. The instructor explained that he should open his reserve parachute. The student then asked what would happen if the reserve parachute didn't open. The instructor replied, "Then you bounce!" The shocked student said, "No way, really?" to which the instructor replied, "Yes way, this ain't Disney World." There are very real consequences in skydiving. If you make a mistake or your equipment malfunctions, you may die. This student had not come to terms with that reality. Even though he was about to jump out of an airplane and fall one hundred twenty miles per hour toward the ground, he hadn't yet fully grasped that there was a chance (and a very big chance if you're careless) that his choices and actions could lead to death. The instructor would have been negligent had he not made that clear.

I think many Christian men suffer from this same blindness about eternity. They go to church and pray before dinner, but they don't really believe that someday we'll all be judged by whether we followed God's commands or not. They're blinded to the reality that we're all going to meet Jesus someday, and He will judge us—and it will be very unpleasant for those who rejected Him. Elijah and Stephen understood this. Stephen even asked God not to hold the sin of the men stoning him against them. He understood that judgment was real and awful. He didn't want the men who were literally killing him to experience the judgment they deserved.

Once you truly understand judgment, it makes it so much easier to follow God when it's hard because you realize the consequences of not following God are just so much worse. Don't be willfully blind to the truth: there are eternal consequences to your choices. You should fear the consequences of not following God so much more than the consequences of not following men. I understand that it's sometimes hard when men are right in front of you and God feels far away, but God is never far away. He's very near and wants you to choose His commands even in the face of intense pressure from men to conform to the world. God loves you and wants to spend eternity with you, but the Bible makes clear He will judge you, and you will spend eternity apart from Him if you don't repent and become a follower of Jesus in this life.

DON'T COMPROMISE ON GOD'S LAW

When God gives a command, you have to follow it. You can't *sort of* follow it or follow *part* of it. You have to follow *all* of it. When God commanded Elijah to go confront kings who could have killed him, Elijah went. He followed God's command. Stephen was fulfilling the Great Commission as he explained to other men that Jesus was the Messiah.[cix] He didn't stop because his life was threatened.

Many men think following all of God's commands makes you rigid and unreasonable. It doesn't. Jesus explained this to His disciples.

> *"Everyone then who hears these words of mine and does them will be like a wise man who built his house on the rock. And the rain fell, and the floods came, and the winds blew and beat on that house, but it did not fall, because it had been founded on the rock. And everyone who hears these words of mine and does not do them will be like a foolish man who built his house on the sand. And the rain fell, and the floods came, and the winds blew and beat against that house, and it fell, and great was the fall of it." (Matthew 7:24-27)*

Jesus made clear that it's wise to follow His commands and it's foolish if you don't. Jesus didn't say, "It's wise to follow My commands unless it's hard . . . or unless it's going to cause tension." Always following God's commands doesn't make you rigid. It makes you wise.

When the Apostles Peter and John were arrested for teaching the people about Jesus, the religious leaders commanded them not to speak about Jesus any further. They refused.[cx] They weren't willing to compromise even if it meant they would be arrested again, which they were. When the religious leaders reminded the apostles they had commanded them not to teach in Jesus' name, they replied, "We must obey God rather than men."[cxi] Peter and John didn't compromise. They were rigid in the eyes of the world but faithful in the eyes of God.

Do you know when you really decide if you're a Christian? It's not when you're at church. It's when you have to decide whether to follow God's commands in the Bible or follow the culture. I often hear men who claim to be Christians say, "I believe in the Bible, except for . . ." and then they list several areas where the Bible and the culture conflict. They're basically saying, "I'll agree with anything in the Bible as long as the culture doesn't object." These are not Christians and certainly not Tough Guys. These are men who are willing to compromise to be acceptable to the culture.

In James 4, the half-brother of Jesus wrote, "Do you not know that friendship with the world is enmity with God? Therefore whoever wishes to be a friend of the world makes himself an enemy of God."[cxii] This is harsh language. If you're trying to please the world, you're literally an enemy of God. You're not just ignoring God. You're someone in direct opposition to

God, fighting against Him. You have to choose between following God or men. There is no compromise where you can satisfy both. The Tough Guys chose God. You should choose God too.

I need to make sure I'm clear about what I'm saying and what I'm not saying. I'm saying, don't compromise on God's commands. I'm not saying, don't compromise in other areas. Don't make the mistake of confusing God's commands with administrative details or preferences. God clearly commanded, "You shall not steal."ᶜˣⁱⁱⁱ God did not command, "You shall not have drums in the church band." I understand you may not like the drums and would prefer to sing hymns accompanied by an organ (or acapella). By all means, find a church that shares that preference. However, don't think you're standing up for God's commands by condemning those churches whose preference is to have a drummer on the worship team (or any other similar area of preference). There are plenty of opportunities to challenge men who are actually compromising on God's commands. You do not need to invent new ones.

TO OBEY IS BETTER THAN TO SACRIFICE

I once heard a pastor of a large church say, "Churches that are strong on mercy and justice are usually weak on righteousness, and churches that are strong on righteousness are usually weak on mercy and justice." I do not think that is universally true since I've attended churches that are strong on both. I think this pastor was making excuses for why his church was weak on righteousness. However, I do think the pastor was reflecting a view held by many men who claim to be Christians. I think there are a lot of men who think they can give more than average (or at least what they think is average) to charities that serve the poor and that effectively earns them the right to ignore some of the commands in the Bible. They wouldn't necessarily say it this clearly, but they say it with their actions. They might volunteer at a soup kitchen and then go home and sleep with their girlfriend. Alternatively, they might give up their Saturdays to tutor kids in a poor neighborhood and then cheat on their tax returns.

The Bible makes it clear that God wants your obedience more than your sacrifice. Samuel gave Saul a command from God to go and fight against the Amalekites and devote everyone, including the animals, to destruction. Instead, Saul left the Amalekite King Agag alive and spared some of the best animals. When Samuel challenged him, Saul said he spared the best animals to sacrifice them to God. Samuel responded:

And Samuel said,
"Has the Lord as great delight in burnt offerings and sacrifices,
as in obeying the voice of the Lord?
Behold, to obey is better than sacrifice,
and to listen than the fat of rams.
For rebellion is as the sin of divination,
and presumption is as iniquity and idolatry.
Because you have rejected the word of the Lord,
he has also rejected you from being king." (1 Samuel 15:22-23)

Saul lost his kingdom because he thought he could make a sacrifice to make up for his disobedience. Don't make this mistake. God doesn't need your sacrifice—He already owns everything. He wants your obedience. God wants you to sacrifice too, but as an act of obedience. He doesn't need you to take care of the poor. He'll use you to help Him take care of the poor if you're obedient. But He'll take care of the poor some other way even if you don't. You're not indispensable. They'll be just fine without you. You may miss out on the blessings you would have received by serving, but you haven't earned the right to anything because of your "sacrifice."

The Tough Guys understood this. Stephen was chosen as one of the first deacons to take care of poor widows among the early Christians. He obviously cared about the poor. However, when he was called to be obedient and proclaim the name of Jesus in front of people who wanted to kill him (and eventually did), he obeyed. He didn't say, "I've done a lot for those poor widows, so I've earned the right to opt out of this difficult situation." Instead, he did what God commanded.

When Nehemiah found out that some of the Jewish nobles and leaders in Judah were taking advantage of other Jews by charging interest or forcing the poor to sell their own children into slavery to wealthier Jews, Nehemiah challenged them, and they stopped. Nehemiah was buying back his Jewish brothers from other nations—where they had been sold into slavery—with his own money. Nehemiah also didn't take the food portions to which he was entitled as governor of Judah. Nehemiah clearly cared about the poor and worked hard to provide for justice for them.[cxiv] But Nehemiah didn't use that as an excuse to ignore God's commands. Nehemiah clearly chose to obey and took on some of the toughest assignments from God.

This idea that God wants obedience more than sacrifice is written over and over throughout the Bible. I put some example verse references below and encourage you to study them.

- Psalm 40:6-8
- Isaiah 1:11-15

- Jeremiah 7:22-23
- Hosea 6:6
- Micah 6:6-8
- Matthew 12:7
- Mark 12:33
- Hebrews 10:5-7

The Tough Guys followed God's commands even when they were hard. You should be generous and sacrifice both your money and your time (which all came from God anyway), but don't use that as an excuse to ignore some of God's commands. Live like the Tough Guys. Choose obedience over sacrifice.

TOUGH GUYS WERE MENTALLY TOUGH

We don't know if all the Tough Guys were physically strong. The Bible doesn't give us enough detail. However, it's clear they were all mentally strong. I often hear men who claim to be Christians say, "We're going to lose" when we're talking about a cultural issue where the country is moving away from God's commands. They have a defeatist attitude. They don't really believe we worship a powerful God who can intervene and change things at any time regardless of the odds that are stacked against us.

The Tough Guys had incredible mental strength. They knew how to perform under pressure. They didn't choke when facing challenging circumstances. They truly believed God was on their side, which gave them the confidence to take action even when the odds seemed stacked against them. Imagine how hard it must have been for Elijah to confront Ahab, who had gone to great lengths to try to find him and kill him? Not only did Elijah confront Ahab, but he also mocked all the false prophets of Baal and Asherah when their false gods failed to send fire. It took mental strength to maintain his resolve.

When Nehemiah decided to rebuild the walls of Jerusalem, he took on a task that other men had been unable to accomplish for almost a hundred years. This didn't deter him. He didn't back down from this incredible challenge. He had the strength to inspire men to help him do something that previously seemed impossible. When Nebuchadnezzar declared all the wise men of Babylon should be killed, Daniel didn't freak out. He didn't run and hide. He responded with prudence and went to the king and asked for an opportunity to interpret his dream.[cxv]

Gideon went into the enemy camp with just his servant. He took on 135,000 men with just three hundred. How strong do you have to be mentally to believe that could work? Gideon clearly had strong faith that gave him his incredible courage and mental toughness.

When the Apostle Paul would arrive in a new city, he would go into the synagogues and debate with the Jewish leaders. He didn't beat around the bush. He went right in and challenged them intellectually. He knew he had truth on his side and wasn't afraid to debate these men even when it often led to someone beating him up or trying to kill him.

Stephen was full of grace and power. When he was brought before the Sanhedrin Council, he likely didn't know he was going to give a sermon that day, but filled with the Holy Spirit, he gave one of the most powerful sermons in the Bible. Stephen didn't cower in the moment; he rose to the occasion and took the opportunity to speak to this influential audience. That took mental toughness.

If you think you have to be physically powerful to be a Tough Guy, that is not the case. These men had a mental toughness that anyone can have regardless of the physique God gave you. The mental toughness to have faith in God when things look bleak is more important than any physical toughness you might have.

When other Christian men tell you, "We're going to lose" some cultural battle, remind them that we worship an all-powerful God. Remind them to have the mental toughness to have faith when things look bleak and believe that we can win any battle with God. Of course, God gets to choose the timing of His actions, but remind these men not to count God out of any fight.

GOD'S LOVE IS UNCONDITIONAL, BUT HIS BLESSING IS NOT

Every good Sunday school teacher in the world has taught his or her students that God loves us unconditionally. God made this clear by sending His only Son to die for us so we may live eternally, but unconditional love does not equal unconditional blessing. Throughout the Bible, God makes clear that His blessing is dependent on our obedience. When God appeared to Solomon after he dedicated the temple, God made it clear.

When I shut up the heavens so that there is no rain, or command the locust to devour the land, or send pestilence among my people, if my people who are called by my name humble themselves, and pray and seek my face and turn from their wicked ways, then I will hear from heaven and will forgive their sin and heal their land. (2 Chronicles 7:13-14)

God will heal our land *if* we obey. This requires prayer, repentance, and obedience. A lot of pastors skip over this point. They focus on the unconditional love a lot since nobody objects to that but downplay the conditional blessings part since that isn't as popular.

This link between obedience and blessing isn't just a theme in the Old Testament. It's repeated in the New Testament as well. After Jesus healed a lame man, He instructed Him not to sin.

Afterward Jesus found him in the temple and said to him, "See, you are well! Sin no more, that nothing worse may happen to you." (John 5:14)

Jesus loved this man enough to heal him, but He also made clear that if the man continued to sin, something worse than being lame could happen to him. Jesus loved him unconditionally but made clear that continued blessing was conditional on the man's obedience. Jesus told him this difficult truth because He loved him. This is another great example of Jesus speaking the truth directly.

The last time I read through the Bible, I wrote down all the verses that tied blessing, prosperity, and flourishing to repentance and obedience. The list of verses is below. I'm not suggesting this is a comprehensive list. These are just the ones I noticed. There are likely more. God made this clear throughout the Bible. He didn't hide it in a footnote; He repeated it over and over.

Genesis 7:1-5	1 Kings 8:25
Genesis 18:17-19	1 Kings 9:4-9
Genesis 22:15-18	1 Kings 11:38
Genesis 26:1-5	2 Kings 21:8
Exodus 15:26	1 Chronicles 28:6-8
Exodus 19:5-6	2 Chronicles 6:14-17
Exodus 20:5-6	2 Chronicles 6:19-40
Exodus 23:20-28	2 Chronicles 7:11-22
Leviticus 26:3-13	2 Chronicles 15:1-4
Numbers 32:15	2 Chronicles 26:5
Numbers 33:55-56	2 Chronicles 27:6

Deuteronomy 4:40

Deuteronomy 5:10

Deuteronomy 5:16

Deuteronomy 5:29

Deuteronomy 5:33

Deuteronomy 6:2-3

Deuteronomy 6:24

Deuteronomy 7:9-15

Deuteronomy 11:13-28

Deuteronomy 12:25-28

Deuteronomy 15:4-18

Deuteronomy 16:15

Deuteronomy 23:20

Deuteronomy 25:15

Deuteronomy 28:1-68

Deuteronomy 29:9

Deuteronomy 30:1-20

Joshua 1:7-8

1 Samuel 12:14-15

1 Kings 2:3-4

Isaiah 56:4-6

Isaiah 57:13

Isaiah 58:7-12

Jeremiah 7:3-7

Jeremiah 22:7-9

Jeremiah 22:15-16

Malachi 2:2

Matthew 5:6

Matthew 5:19

Matthew 6:14

Matthew 6:31-33

Isaiah 3:10

2 Chronicles 28:6

2 Chronicles 30:9

2 Chronicles 33:8

2 Chronicles 34:26-28

Ezra 9:12

Nehemiah 1:8-9

Nehemiah 9:28-31

Nehemiah 13:17-18

Psalm 1:3

Psalm 41:1-3

Psalm 81:13-16

Psalm 89:30-32

Psalm 91:9-10

Psalm 112:1-3

Psalm 132:12

Proverbs 3:9-10

Proverbs 3:33-34

Isaiah 1:19

1 Kings 3:14

1 Kings 6:11-13

Isaiah 48:18-19

Mark 10:29-30

Luke 2:14

John 5:14

John 14:21-23

John 15:10-14

Romans 2:10

Romans 8:28

Ephesians 6:1-3

Ephesians 6:5-8

Hebrews 12:14

James 4:6

Some people are offended by this truth. It makes them think God is only about rules. That's clearly not true and has become an excuse for them to do what is right in their own eyes. The Tough Guys understood that we should fear God so that things will go well with us. This clearly doesn't mean you're going to have an easy life on earth. Stephen was stoned to death for challenging the Jewish leaders. Elijah lived out in the wilderness, and God had to have birds bring him food (which is disgusting and at the same time, really awesome). JTB had his head cut off (which I'm pretty sure is actually less awful than being stoned, although I would prefer not to find out). Alternatively, Gideon acquired wealth and power after following God's commands, and David became a wealthy king and lived to an old age. Your blessing and prosperity may come in this life or through rewards in heaven, which are worth so much more than any earthly reward. Live like the Tough Guys and follow God's commands so that you will be blessed.

TRUE TEST OF FAITH

The true test of your faith is not what you do when you're around other Christians, it's what you do when you're not. It's easy to be a Christian in church. When you're surrounded by other men who agree with you, of course you fear God. But here's the question: *Do you fear God when you're surrounded by men who don't fear God?*

Stephen was part of the community of early Christians. He was chosen as a leader. In that setting, he was surrounded by men who followed Jesus. It would have been easy to fear God, but when Stephen was later surrounded by men who didn't fear God, he didn't waver. He didn't cave in. He didn't soften his message to avoid upsetting men. In short, he didn't fear the men who were threatening him. He chose to fear God. You may think that was dumb since he lost his life. However, we're still talking about him two thousand years later. How many men who went along with the crowd have had that kind of long-term impact on the world?

There is no record of Elijah having a community. He seemed to be a loner, but the Bible records his interactions with God, so he wasn't alone. When Elijah spoke with God in the wilderness, it would have been easy to fear Him. There often weren't any other men around to fear anyway. But when Elijah did confront kings, he was the only one present who believed in God when he challenged them.[50] Like Stephen, he didn't waver. He feared God even when surrounded by men who wanted to kill him.

---

50. Alone among men. God was with him.

God designed you to follow Him. In Matthew 12:30, Jesus said, "Whoever is not with me is against me, and whoever does not gather with me scatters." There is no Switzerland with God. You can't thread the needle by trying to please both the culture and God. You're either all in or you're all out. God doesn't allow 90 percent of a person into heaven. It's all or nothing. This problem is nothing new.

> *Nevertheless, many even of the authorities believed in him [Jesus], but for fear of the Pharisees they did not confess it, so that they would not be put out of the synagogue; for they loved the glory that comes from man more than the glory that comes from God. (John 12:42-43)*

Even though some of the Jewish leaders believed in Jesus, they wanted the praise of their peers more than praise from God. It's not enough to just believe that God is real. You have to submit to Him and choose Him over the approval of men. The Tough Guys were willing to forgo the praise of men to serve God instead. You should too.

HUMILITY VS. TIMIDITY

The Bible commands us to be humble.[cxvi] For many men, that word has a negative connotation. It sounds like an instruction to be weak, but humility is not the same as timidity. God doesn't call us to be timid. He wants us to submit to His will and His commands. That's what's meant by the call to be humble: to be humble before God.

The life of Moses illustrated this. God called Moses the most humble man on the earth. In fact, since Moses was so humble God spoke to him face to face instead of through dreams.[cxvii] I should point out that Moses wrote this about himself, which doesn't seem like a very humble thing to do; but the Bible is inspired by the Holy Spirit, so let's assume Moses didn't write this out of pride.

Even though Moses was humble, he was not timid. Moses challenged Pharaoh to let the Israelites go. He led the Israelites for forty years through the desert. Moses wasn't afraid to challenge God not to wipe out the Israelites after they built the golden calf. He also commanded the execution of three thousand of his fellow Israelites for their sin.[cxviii] Moses also led the Israelites in battle against the Midianites.[cxix] Moses was bold and courageous. He wasn't weak even though he submitted his life to God's will. In fact, it took incredible strength to humble himself and serve God when it was so risky.

The other Tough Guys had humility and yet were not timid. Elijah submitted his life to God yet was bold enough to mock the false god Baal right in front of his four hundred fifty prophets. Stephen submitted his life to God yet was bold enough to call out the Jewish leaders for their hypocrisy and blindness. Gideon was humble enough to submit to God's commands when they seemed crazy (fight 135,000 with three hundred) and yet courageous enough to go and fight. Nehemiah had humility and yet he pulled out the hair of Jewish leaders who were exploiting their countrymen. These were not weak men.

Having humility doesn't mean we don't take action or that we fail to challenge other men. It doesn't mean we aren't bold. In fact, God wants us to be bold. King David was incredibly bold (taking on a giant with a slingshot would give you some street cred), and God called him a man after His own heart.[cxx] God wants us to use the skills and talents He's given us to lead our families, disciple other men, and serve our communities. However, He also wants us to submit our lives and our will to Him.

I'm old enough that I grew up watching *Little House on the Prairie*. (There were only three stations back then, so I had the choice to watch that, *Fantasy Island*, or *Columbo*, and my mom wouldn't let me watch *Fantasy Island* or *Columbo*). Michael Landon played Charles Ingalls, who was the father of the main character, Laura Ingalls. In the show, Charles was portrayed as a humble man who feared God and worked hard on his farm to provide for his family; but it seemed like every four or five episodes, some guy was being unreasonable, and Charles had to punch him right in the face. Typically, the guy would wise up, figure out he was wrong and, in the end, appreciate that Charles had knocked some sense into him. Now, television isn't real life, and I'm not suggesting you go around punching guys (unless they really deserve it). But the show did a good job of portraying a man who was both humble and bold. He submitted his life to God but was also courageous. He didn't back down from challenging other men. Charles Ingalls would have been a Tough Guy even though he was just a humble farmer who lived in a little house on the prairie.

Don't ever think that humility equals weakness or timidity. When you choose to submit your life to God like the Tough Guys, you will likely find that your courage and boldness increases, and God can use you to do even more than you ever thought possible.

TOUGH GUYS FOLLOWED GOD WHEN IT WAS HUMILIATING

Fearing God sometimes means tolerating personal humiliation. While this may seem outwardly weak, it actually takes incredible strength to follow God when you know the world will mock you. You need incredible confidence to intentionally do something humiliating.

God commanded the prophet Hosea to marry a woman who would cheat on him repeatedly and eventually leave him. But it gets even better for Hosea because God later commanded him to take her back, which required purchasing her out of slavery. This is not every mother's dream for her son.

While this was humiliating to Hosea, God used this as an example of how the people of Israel cheated on Him with other gods and yet He promised He would redeem them.^{cxxi} Can you imagine how Hosea felt? When his wife finally left, he probably thought, *Good riddance.* Then when God commanded him to redeem her, Hosea must have thought, *You have got to be kidding me. It was humiliating enough the first time. Now I have to do it again?* Yet Hosea still feared God and did as He commanded.

Potiphar put Joseph in prison for a false accusation of rape. Joseph could have given in to the advances of Potiphar's wife, but he followed God's commands instead. Joseph spent many years in prison and endured its humiliation because he feared God.

When King David brought the Ark to Jerusalem, he danced before the Ark in a linen ephod. The passage in 2 Samuel 6 suggests David exposed himself as he danced. First of all, if you had to look up the word *ephod*, you are not alone. As best I can tell, it's basically a sleeveless dress that priests wore. So David wore some strange clothing to celebrate God. Second of all, David danced. If you are a man, anytime you dance, it is humiliating. (I'm sorry if you disagree, but you are wrong.) Third of all, David exposed himself, which is really humiliating. This story makes me really appreciate the guy who invented underwear, which wasn't apparently until the 1930s. That guy doesn't get enough credit. Many would disagree with me, but I would put underwear right up there with the light bulb in terms of most important inventions in the last two hundred years.

When David's wife Michal scolded him for exposing himself, David explained that he danced before the Lord. David cared more about pleasing God than maintaining his dignity before men.

God made Ezekiel mute so he could only speak when he gave a prophecy from God. He also made Ezekiel lie on his side for more than a year.^{cxxii} This would have been humiliating (and painful!), but Ezekiel chose to follow God and not worry about what men thought about him.

Not long after Jesus' ascension into heaven, the apostles were preaching at the temple. The Jewish leaders had them beaten (which was both painful and humiliating) and instructed them not to preach the name of Jesus. The apostles left and rejoiced that they were worthy to suffer dishonor for the name of Jesus.[cxxiii] The apostles didn't mind the humiliation before men. They were excited that God chose them to suffer this humiliation to honor the name of Jesus. Imagine if more Christian men had that attitude today.

The Tough Guys had a healthy fear of God that was much stronger than their fear of men. They chose to follow God's commands even when it meant personal humiliation. The joy of pleasing God overshadowed any embarrassment they felt from men. You should resolve to be like the Tough Guys and follow God even when it's personally humiliating.

Chapter 21

PASTOR'S LOG: WARLORDS AND HERETICS

DOUG: TACKLING HERESY IN THE CHURCH

After serving twenty years in the military, Doug[51] decided to attend seminary and pursue a role as a pastor. He was part of a large Christian denomination, and after seminary, he was asked to lead a church in a part of the country where he and his wife didn't know anyone. After visiting, Doug felt God had called him there, so he took the role. He and his wife started to get engaged in the community and the life of the congregation of about three hundred people.

After a few years, some churches in Doug's denomination started to deny the authority of Scripture and insert their own beliefs in place of the clear commands and truths of the Bible. Churches within the denomination who still believed in the authority of Scripture had to wrestle with how to address these heresies. Doug wrestled with it as well.

Initially, the heresies were limited to certain groups of churches, and Doug felt that as long as his church continued to preach the truth of Scripture, he could shepherd the congregation well. He also felt that the churches who continued to preach truth could influence the churches teaching heresy to return to the truth of the Bible. However, over time, more and more churches in the denomination began to embrace the heresies. Doug spent a few years trying to encourage his denomination to return to

51. Pseudonym used to protect the individual's identity.

the truth of the Bible, but even striving alongside others who agreed with him, he was unsuccessful.

A regional leader of his denomination was scheduled to visit, so Doug set up a time for the congregation to meet with him and ask questions. The congregation asked the leader about some of the heresies, and Doug quickly realized this leader, who had authority over his church, was also believing and teaching heresies. For instance, one congregant asked about the bodily resurrection of Jesus, and the leader responded by saying he believed the tomb was empty, but we don't know how. The leader was denying the bodily resurrection of Jesus, which is incredibly clear in the Bible and is also central to Christian belief. If God didn't conquer death through the resurrection of Jesus, we're all in a lot of trouble.

Another congregant asked if the leader believed that "Jesus was the way, and the truth and the life" as it says clearly in John 14. The leader responded by saying that Jesus said those words to Thomas, so that was only true for Thomas. It was clear this leader no longer believed in the clear truths of the Bible.

Doug was shocked by the open heresy and realized he could no longer serve under that leader. With more churches in the denomination openly teaching heresy, Doug realized he had to leave. Around the same time, a group within his church approached him about leaving to form a new church outside the denomination so they would be free to teach the truth of the Bible.

Doug left his role as lead pastor of a church of three hundred to launch a church plant. This is incredibly challenging for a pastor. First of all, it's hard to launch a new church—most of them fail. In addition, it's typically financially challenging unless you have donors who support you until the church is larger and congregational giving is sufficient to support all the expenses of the church. A church plant typically can't even afford to fully fund one pastor's salary out of the initial giving; they require external support. In addition, Doug and his wife were living far away from their families. Most of their local relationships were in the old church. They didn't have a local network of family and friends who could help them. They had to rely on God and the small group in this new congregation. In addition, this was already a second career for Doug who was in his fifties. Most churches who look for new pastors prefer that they're in their thirties or forties (yes, there is age discrimination even in Christianity). If the church plant failed, Doug would have limited opportunities to lead other churches.

Despite the typical challenges, God blessed Doug and this new church. From day one, the congregation gave enough to cover his salary and all the other expenses of the church. In addition, the church has been able to give a 10 percent tithe of their giving to other ministries each year.

They quickly found another church willing to rent them space to hold their services, and just a few years later, a Christian real estate developer offered to sell them a church he had recently purchased for the same price that he'd paid for it—and he included a ten-thousand-dollar donation to help them renovate the interior. In just a few years, the giving at the new church had grown enough to allow them to take him up on his generous offer and purchase a permanent building.

Doug has led that new church for more than seventeen years. God has provided everything they've needed. While the church is smaller than his previous church, they've never had financial challenges since the people have always been generous. Doug has been able to lead this congregation and challenge them to live out the truth of the Bible. God has blessed his new ministry and allowed him to lead people away from the teachings of heretics.

Unfortunately, the challenges Doug faced are all too common in our country. Heresy is on the rise in many churches and denominations. Tough Guys are needed to challenge their churches to end their heresies or, if they refuse, to lead other men away from those churches. Resolve in your mind to follow Doug's example and challenge heresy. Trust that God can provide the things you need to disciple men to follow Him.

JOEL DEHART: TRUSTING GOD ENOUGH TO LOVE YOUR ENEMIES

Joel[52] grew up in Pakistan as a missionary kid. He learned about the Muslim culture there and spoke the local languages. As an adult, he taught English in Islamabad as he worked for a Christian aid organization.

One summer, Joel offered to serve as a translator for a veterinarian from Texas who wanted to offer animal health training and vaccinations in Afghanistan (because who doesn't enjoy a good trip to hostile third-world nations). This was long before the U.S. went to war in Afghanistan, but the country was no less hostile to Christians. To most men in America, going to Afghanistan to help teach people to care for their animals probably sounds crazy. For Joel, it was natural given his upbringing in that part of the world and the attitude of service instilled in him by his missionary parents. Joel had a heart to share the good news of Jesus with Muslims. He trusted that God would protect him even in a hostile country.

Toward the end of their trip, an Afghan warlord took Joel and the veterinarian hostage and demanded a ransom for their release. They were soon separated, and Joel spent most of his captivity alone with Afghans who were guarding him. The veterinarian was released after three months, but Joel was held captive for six months before he was released. During that

---

52. You can read Joel's entire story in his book *The Upper Hand: God's Sovereignty in Afghan Captivity.*

time, he was moved several times and stayed in homes where he slept on the floor and didn't have running water. He often went weeks without baths. He had to pick fleas and lice off his clothing. The warlord who abducted him constantly lied to justify his kidnapping and gave him little indication about when he would be released. In addition to the frustration of losing his freedom and the uncertainty of whether he might be harmed or killed, Joel had to live in conditions most Americans (including me) would find appalling. A one-star motel would be luxury compared to what Joel endured.

What impressed me about Joel's story was how he showed his captors the love of Jesus even while they had taken his freedom. Joel taught his captors and some of their kids English. He shared the gospel with those who were preventing him from returning home. He helped them with household chores like cooking, collecting firewood, and building projects. He even continued to translate prescriptions from the veterinarian to help provide medicine for both his captors and their animals. Joel trusted God enough to love his captors even as they committed this injustice against him.

It's not that Joel was happy with his situation. He prayed for his release. He wrestled with God, trying to understand why he was kidnapped. Many days he prayed that he would be released that day and it didn't happen, but Joel continued to trust God throughout his captivity. He believed that God would get him through it alive. He spent time praying and singing hymns. When he was finally given a small portion of the Bible, he would read it over and over to meditate on God's Word. When people would show him small acts of kindness, he would praise God. Once, someone gave Joel nail clippers, and he praised God because that was exactly what he needed. Can you imagine praising God for something as simple as nail clippers? Joel did. He knew God was providing what he needed when he needed it.

One of the many impressive things about Joel's story is that he was able to build many relationships with the people who lived in the towns where he was held captive. As a result of his belief that God was in charge, he was able to function in a way that was outwardly focused on others rather than inwardly focused on his own problems. When I read some of his journal entries during his captivity, I was struck by how freeing it must have been to trust God during that ordeal. The daily uncertainty and fear of not knowing what would happen to you could be paralyzing, but because Joel trusted God, he was able to build relationships and focus on an outward mission. Fearing God rather than men is a biblical command, but at a practical level it's also completely liberating. It allows you to function without the constant stress of worrying what will happen to you. Joel's story is a great example of how to fear God in a difficult situation. Throughout his ordeal, Joel trusted that God was in charge and nothing could happen to him unless God allowed it.

Chapter 22

JESUS WAS GOD YET HE FEARED GOD

J esus was (and is) God as a member of the Trinity, so it doesn't seem as if
He would need to fear God. Yet He did. Jesus submitted His life to God
despite constant threats from men. The Apostle Paul explained this in his
letter to the Philippians.

> *Let each of you look not only to his own interests, but also to the interests
> of others. Have this mind among yourselves, which is yours in Christ
> Jesus, who, though he was in the form of God, did not count equality
> with God a thing to be grasped, but emptied himself, by taking the
> form of a servant, being born in the likeness of men. And being found
> in human form, he humbled himself by becoming obedient to the point
> of death, even death on a cross. (Philippians 2:4-8)*

Jesus submitted His life to God. He was obedient even when it led to
His physical death in a humiliating way. What's incredible is Jesus understood
all of this well in advance. He explained to his disciples repeatedly that He
would have to die, although they didn't understand what He was telling
them. Imagine knowing that you were going to be beaten and executed in a
gruesome way for years in advance and yet still serving God? It would be so
difficult. You would want to run away like Jonah, but Jesus didn't run. He
continued His mission and submitted to the will of God.

Jesus didn't want to suffer and die. Right before He was arrested, He made a final appeal to God. He asked God to "remove this cup from me," but still said, "not my will, but yours be done."[cxxiv] Jesus wasn't a masochist. He didn't want to suffer pain and humiliation any more than we do, but nevertheless, He feared God and submitted to Him. He understood that God's plan was better than His.

Jesus had practiced submitting to God long before His crucifixion. At the beginning of His ministry, Jesus fasted forty days in the wilderness while Satan tempted Him. If you've ever fasted, you know that you get weak quickly. After forty days of fasting, you're incredibly weak. Satan tried to get Jesus to bow down to him. Satan wanted Jesus to fear him more than He feared God. Jesus refused. He was full of the Holy Spirit and even in His bodily weakness refused to submit to Satan.[cxxv]

Satan offered Jesus the whole world, and yet He refused to submit to Satan. How often do Christian men give in for so much less? Christian men often give in for a promotion or a night of promiscuity or fifteen minutes of fame. Jesus was offered so much more, and He still said no. He still feared God more than . . . not just man, but Satan.

Those are just the temptations. That doesn't include the threats. If men are threatening to do you economic or physical harm if you obey God, do you fear them or do you fear God? Jesus showed us how to fear God in the most difficult circumstances.

In the Bible, Jesus was threatened by men, but He was also tempted directly by Satan. Satan used men and even entered into Judas to get him to betray Jesus.[cxxvi] Satan is still using men today to tempt us and pull us away from God. When you find yourself fearing men who pressure you to disobey God, remember that it is Satan who is pulling the strings. Follow the example of Jesus and don't give in to the schemes of the devil. Fear God and He will reward you—either in this life or in the life to come. Either way, you won't regret fearing God more than the men who are filled by Satan.

CONCLUSION:
LIVE LIKE THE TOUGH GUYS
AND HELP SAVE OUR NATION

O ur nation is in trouble, but it's not too late. We can turn our nation back to God. We can challenge people to repent and conform their lives to God's commands. A great way to start is to challenge the men already in our churches to live like the Tough Guys. That starts with some tough love and brutal honesty. We need to explain to men that it's not easy to truly give your life to Jesus. However, God will give you the strength to live for Him and make other men into disciples.

This false narrative, that being a Christian is easy, is simply not an effective way to convince men to seriously evaluate the claims of the Bible. Men don't want to join a team that sets the bar really low for its members. Who wants to join a sports team that says, "Let's try to come in fourth"? Who wants to invest in a team that makes practice optional and only a few people show up? Similarly, why would strong men join a church where members routinely ignore biblical commands, and no one challenges them to live in accordance with those commands? What a waste of time to show up every Sunday and listen to a bunch of words most people will just ignore the minute they walk out the door. Who wants to join that team? I can ignore things from the comfort of my own living room—or better yet, while I sleep in. I don't need to go to church every Sunday and give them a bunch of money for the opportunity to listen to things everyone will ignore. It reeks of hypocrisy, and it's a waste of time. Men don't want to join a hypocritical team, especially one that wastes their time and money.

We need to make clear to men outside the Church that it's really hard to truly give your life to Jesus. If you want to recruit men to do something, don't tell them it's easy. Tell them it's hard. That is much more likely to engage them than saying it's easy. If they choose to follow God, He will give them all the toughness they need to withstand the pressures of the culture and the schemes of Satan.

We wrote this book to highlight what it looks like when men truly follow God. We wanted to highlight their strength and courage. We also wanted to be honest about their struggles and sacrifices. It takes a really strong man to live like a true Christian. We need to use that message to challenge men both inside and outside the Church.

If you're not yet a Christian, don't reject Jesus because of weak men inside the Church. Evaluate the lives of the strongest Christians. Evaluate the life of Jesus. Read the truth of the Bible for yourself. Truly following Jesus will be the hardest and most masculine thing you could ever do. We encourage you to consider giving your life to Jesus and joining the ranks of the other Tough Guys.

If you're already following Jesus, we hope this book has challenged you to take any part of your life that you were holding back and submit it to God. Go all in and live like the Tough Guys. As you challenge other men to consider the claims of the Bible, don't tell them it's easy. Point to the lives of the Tough Guys. Tell them the truth: it's hard, but if they submit to God, He will give them the strength to follow Him. More importantly, point to the life of Jesus. Explain how He was (and is) the ultimate Tough Guy. Show them why they should want to emulate His life and follow Him. Live like the Tough Guys and make disciples that follow all of Jesus' commands.

If more men start to live like the Tough Guys, we can turn our nation back to God. If we repent and return to God, He has promised to hear our prayers and heal our land. Join the ranks of the Tough Guys and help us save our nation.

ENDNOTES

i. Matthew 16:24

ii. Abraham took Keturah as a wife, although it's not clear if this happened before or after Sarah died. Genesis 25:1.

iii. Genesis 25:2

iv. Genesis 36:12

v. Acts 20:7-12

vi. 2 Timothy 4:6-8

vii. Acts 9:1-2

viii. Galatians 2:11-14

ix. Acts 9:16

x. Judges 6:15

xi. Genesis 25:23

xii. 1 Samuel 16:11-12

xiii. Judges 6:16

xiv. Judges 6:34

xv. 1 Samuel 16:13

xvi. Exodus 4:10

xvii. Judges 8:24-26

xviii. Judges 8:32

xix. 2 Kings 2:11

xx. Judges 6

xxi. 1 Corinthians 2:3

xxii. Nehemiah 2:2

xxiii. Exodus 4:1-17

xxiv. Exodus 24; Exodus 34

xxv. Exodus 33:15-16

xxvi. 1 Kings 19:14

xxvii. Daniel 6:10

xxviii. Nehemiah 1:4

xxix. 1 Thessalonians 5:17

xxx. George Reginald Balleine, *A History of the Evangelical Party in the Church of England* (London: Longmans, Green, and Co., 1908).

xxxi. David Wilkerson, Elizabeth Sherrill, and John Sherrill, *The Cross and the Switchblade* (New York: Penguin Group, 1986).

xxxii. Arthur T. Pierson, George Muller of Bristol (New York: Fleming H. Revell Company, 1899).

xxxiii. 2 Chronicles 15

xxxiv. 2 Chronicles 16

xxxv. Martin Luther King Jr., *The Autobiography of Martin Luther King Jr,* Clayborne Carson Ed. (New York: Grand Central Publishing, 1998), 344.

xxxvi. John 7:5

xxxvii. Mark 6:1-6

xxxviii. Acts 1:14

xxxix. Jeremiah 52:28

xl. Daniel 1:3-7

xli. Daniel 1:8-16

xlii. Daniel 2:1-49. The story was very similar to how Joseph was put in charge of Egypt, which we'll address later in the book.

xliii. Daniel 6:1-24

xliv. Daniel 4:19

xlv. Daniel 4:28-33

xlvi. Daniel 5:29

xlvii. Daniel 5:30-31

xlviii. Luke 1:17

xlix. Mark 6:17-18

l. Matthew 14:3-5

li. Luke 3:16

lii. James 1:5-8

liii. Daniel 4:27.

liv. Matthew 3:5-6

lv. Daniel 2:16

lvi. Jonah 1:3

lvii. Jonah 3:10 – 4:2, 4:11

lviii. Jeremiah 1:6

lix. Jeremiah 20:7-9

lx. Jeremiah 26:20-23

lxi. Matthew 10:34-35

lxii. Isaiah 55:11

lxiii. Number 4:1-15, 7:9

lxiv. 2 Samuel 6:1-7

lxv. Proverbs 27:17

lxvi. George Marsden, *A Short Life of Jonathan Edwards* (Grand Rapids: William B. Eerdmans Publishing Company, 2008).

lxvii. Genesis 19:24-25; Luke 17:28-29

lxviii. Matthew 5:44

lxix. Matthew 16:21-23

lxx. Matthew 16:24

lxxi. John 6:67

lxxii. Genesis 39:2-6

lxxiii. Genesis 39:23

lxxiv. Nehemiah 2

lxxv. Nehemiah 3-4

lxxvi. Nehemiah 5

lxxvii. Nehemiah 9-10

lxxviii. Nehemiah 13

lxxix. Nehemiah 6

lxxx. 1 Corinthians 6

lxxxi. Galatians 4

lxxxii. https://christianhistoryinstitute.org/magazine/article/ministry-in-killing-fields

lxxxiii. Genesis 39:1-6

lxxxiv. Genesis 39:21-23

lxxxv. Nehemiah 2

ENDNOTES

lxxxvi. Daniel 2

lxxxvii. Daniel 6

lxxxviii. Genesis 2:15

lxxxix. Jeremiah 1:6

xc. 1 Samuel 17

xci. *https://www.sports-reference.com/cbb/coaches/john-wooden-1.html

   *https://www.britannica.com/biography/John-Wooden

   *https://hofbbplayers.com/john-wooden/

   *https://www2.indstate.edu/news/news.php?newsid=346

   *https://www.indystar.com/story/sports/college/2017/03/15/private-pain-clarence-walker/99144560/

   *https://www.tribstar.com/news/lifestyles/john-wooden-built-the-foundation-for-his-legacy-at-indiana-state-teachers-college/article_308e883e-741f-5295-bbb2-9c15b43845b7.html

   *Pat Williams with David Wimbish, *How to Be Like Coach Wooden* (Deerfield Beach, FL: Health Communications, Inc., 2006).

xcii. 1 Kings 17:1

xciii. 1 Kings 18:10

xciv. 1 Kings 18:19-20

xcv. 1 Kings 18:23

xcvi. 1 Kings 18:19

xcvii. 1 Kings 18:33-35

xcviii. 1 Kings 18:40

xcix. 2 Kings 1:2

c. 2 Kings 1:3-4

ci. 2 Kings 1:9

cii. 2 Kings 1:12

ciii. 2 King 1:11

civ. 2 Kings 1:12

cv. 2 Kings 1:13

cvi. 2 Kings 1:13-14

cvii. 2 Kings 1:15-16

cviii. 1 John 4:8

cix. Matthew 28

cx. Acts 4

cxi. Acts 5:29

cxii. James 4:4

cxiii. Exodus 20:15

cxiv. Nehemiah 5

cxv. Daniel 2

cxvi. 1 Peter 5:6; Philippians 2:3-11; James 4:6

cxvii. Numbers 12

cxviii. Exodus 32

cxix. Numbers 31

cxx. 1 Samuel 13:14

cxxi. Hosea 1-3

cxxii. Ezekiel 3-4

cxxiii. Acts 5:41

cxxiv. Luke 22:42

cxxv. Luke 4

cxxvi. John 13:27

CPSIA information can be obtained
at www.ICGtesting.com
Printed in the USA
BVHW040238270821
615258BV00004B/16